| DATE | | | |
|---|---|---|---|
|  |  |  |  |
|  |  |  |  |
|  |  |  |  |
|  |  |  |  |
|  |  |  |  |
|  |  |  |  |
|  |  |  |  |
|  |  |  |  |
|  |  |  |  |
|  |  |  |  |
|  |  |  |  |
|  |  |  |  |
|  |  |  |  |

# TWENTIETH CENTURY VIEWS

The aim of this series is to present the best in contemporary critical opinion on major authors, providing a twentieth century perspective on their changing status in an era of profound revaluation.

Maynard Mack, *Series Editor*
Yale University

# THE THEATER OF
# BLACK AMERICANS

VOLUME II

# THE THEATER OF
# BLACK AMERICANS

## VOLUME II

*The Presenters: Companies of Players*
*The Participators: Audiences and Critics*

### A COLLECTION OF CRITICAL ESSAYS

Edited by
*Errol Hill*

Prentice-Hall, Inc.  *Englewood Cliffs, N.J.*

*Library of Congress Cataloging in Publication Data*

Main entry under title:

THE THEATER OF BLACK AMERICANS.

    (Twentieth century views)   (A Spectrum Book)
    Bibliography: p.
    CONTENTS: v. 1. Roots and rituals. The image
makers.  v. 2. The presenters. The participators.
      1.  Afro-American theater—Addresses, essays,
lectures.  I.  Hill, Errol.
PN2270.A35T48     792'.0973      79-16658
ISBN 0-13-912733-X (v. 2)
ISBN 0-13-912725-9 (v. 2) pbk.

Editorial/production supervision by Eric Newman
Cover illustration by Stanley Wyatt
Manufacturing buyers: Cathie Lenard and Barbara A. Frick

10  9  8  7  6  5  4  3  2  1

PRENTICE-HALL INTERNATIONAL, INC. *(London)*
PRENTICE-HALL OF AUSTRALIA PTY. LIMITED *(Sydney)*
PRENTICE-HALL OF CANADA, LTD. *(Toronto)*
PRENTICE-HALL OF INDIA PRIVATE LIMITED *(New Delhi)*
PRENTICE-HALL OF JAPAN, INC. *(Tokyo)*
PRENTICE-HALL OF SOUTHEAST ASIA PTE. LTD. *(Singapore)*
WHITEHALL BOOKS LIMITED *(Wellington, New Zealand)*

# Contents

# THE THEATER OF
# BLACK AMERICANS

VOLUME II

# Introduction

*by Errol Hill*

Theatre is both an art and an industry; an expression of culture and a source of livelihood for artists and craftsmen; a medium of instruction and a purveyor of entertainment. The essays collected in this book attempt to view Black theatre in all these aspects, but the exercise goes beyond the purely academic. There is a sense of urgency that informs our inquiry. Black Americans today recognize, perhaps more clearly than at any other time in their history, that theatre as an institution can have a significant impact on the relentless struggle of a deprived racial minority for full equality and on the need for spiritual well-being of a people divorced from their ancestral heritage through centuries of degrading slavery. The trend is clearly marked in the spectacular growth of Black theatres across the country.

Widespread recognition of the theatre's potential for changing, healing, and restoring—a return as it were, to the pristine function of the communal, ritual drama—has thrown the Afro-American theatre into a flurry of controversy. The positions taken by theorists and practitioners serve only to generate further questions that call forth still more manifestoes. What, for instance, should be the principal objective of Black theatre? Should its content be strictly defined by the overriding concern for Black liberation? To what audience should this theatre be addressed primarily? What form should it take? How may it express a Black identity, if such a characteristic does in fact exist? What price art in Black theatre when Black people are involved in a struggle for survival? What is the true role of the critic in this theatre? These and many similar crucial questions provide a salutary philosophical counterpoint to the proliferating and sometimes frenzied activities of Black theatre groups nationwide.

It is well to remind ourselves that these issues are not new to Black theatre, though they have never before had a national forum nor have they been voiced with such force and pressure, a force and pressure due in no small part to the Black revolutionary context in which they have lately been raised. Others in earlier decades—most notably during the period of the 1920s commonly referred to as the Harlem Renaissance—have wrestled with similar questions. But the rapid decline of European colonialism in Africa since the 1950s and the concomitant emergence of Black nation states, the 1954 Supreme Court order requiring public school desegregation coupled with civil rights battles on the home front, and the rallying cry for immediate equality by outspoken leaders such as Martin Luther King and Malcolm X— all have contributed to the recent explosion of Black nationalist sentiment in the arts. Contributing too to a heightened concern with the nature and scope of Black theatre are the increased concentration of Black Americans in urban areas and the Black Arts movement with its emphasis on Black cultural centers in which revolutionary political action and community organization are paired with poetry, drama, and the arts. Culture in this context becomes central to the struggle rather than peripheral. The arts become the means for reaching the public, and as a result the theatre, being the most public of the arts, finds itself in the forefront of the nationalist movement.

Back in 1858 William Wells Brown chose the dramatic form for his public addresses against slavery. It was in 1915, however, that the programmatic use of Black drama as an instrument for social reform was begun by the National Association for the Advancement of Colored People. That year, the NAACP appointed a Drama Committee to study ways and means of utilizing the stage in the service of its cause. Chief among the members of this Committee was W. E. B. DuBois, who, in 1900, had predicted that the relationship between the darker and lighter races of man would be the chief problem of the twentieth century. A Harvard Ph.D. and Professor of Economics and History at Atlanta University, DuBois joined the NAACP in 1910 and founded its magazine, *The Crisis,* which he edited for twenty-four years. From this platform he led the militant wing of the Negro movement and spoke out fearlessly against racial discrimination of every kind. The intention of the Drama Committee was not simply to sponsor a rash of propaganda plays that spoke in one-sided accents of current social problems. DuBois was too much of an intellectual and statesman for such a simple-minded approach. He had earlier published *The Souls of Black Folk*, one of the first examinations of Black arts, and on the occasion of the 1913 Exposition to observe fifty years of emancipation from slavery, he had written and staged a pageant, *The Star of Ethiopia.* Two years later he reflected on that experience:

> In art and literature we should try to loose the tremendous emotional wealth of the Negro and the dramatic strength of his problems through writing, the stage, pageantry, and other forms of art. We should resurrect forgotten ancient Negro art and history and we should set the black man before the world as both a creative artist and a strong subject for artistic treatment.[1]

The urgent need, then, was to develop good Black dramatists writing about the Black experience and to assure them a hearing on the dramatic stage. In the first decades of this century, when Blacks were effectively shut out from the legitimate professional theatre, the Lafayette Players in 1915 courageously set up shop in Harlem to prove that Black actors were as competent at their craft as their White counterparts downtown. Hardly had the Players begun their long and noteworthy career of staging mostly Broadway revivals in condensed versions when protests began to flow from the pens of Black critics. The Broadway theatre might ignore honest portrayals of Black life and culture, but a Harlem-based theatre imitating alien Broadway fare was not to be silently tolerated.

Lovett Fort-Whiteman, drama editor of *The Messenger*, affirming that the stage for Negroes should be dominated by Negroes, demanded that "our society be reflected upon the American stage even if we have to call a mass meeting of Harlem's theatregoers and effect a boycott on the Lafayette Theatre."[2] The Players attempted to meet this harsh criticism by offering a prize for original Black plays, but there is no evidence that this action produced a radical change in their repertory. It was left to Du-

[1] *The Crisis,* IX (April, 1915), p. 312.
[2] *The Messenger,* vol. 1, no. 11 (November, 1917), p. 30.

Bois, as editor of the magazine *The Crisis,* to initiate the Krigwa Playwriting Contest in 1925, which resulted in the publication of several prizewinning short plays, the emergence of new Black playwrights, male and female, and the founding of the Krigwa Little Theatre intended as a nationwide Black theatre movement. This was in the midst of the Harlem Renaissance, when Black leaders spoke with a new assertiveness of their needs and aspirations. In theatre, the sparkling Black musical comedy represented by *Shuffle Along* took Broadway by storm. Not all Blacks rejoiced at this conquest. Broadway, after all, was a White preserve patronized by White audiences, and the Black Broadway-type musical comedy for all its flair and vigor was still too reminiscent of the despised minstrel tradition for everyone's comfort. In 1926, having formed the Harlem group of Krigwa Players, DuBois enunciated his four fundamental principles for a Negro theatre. Such a theatre, he asserted, had to be *about us, by us, for us,* and *near us* (that is, located in the Black community).[3]

The Krigwa Players established themselves in the basement of the 135th Street Harlem Library, which they helped to convert into a pocket theatre for their productions and which was occupied by successive companies of Harlem theatres after the Krigwa group became inactive in 1930. Their first season opened with three one-act plays by prizewinning authors of *The Crisis* competition. They were careful to eschew the separatism and exclusivity that in the '60s hobbled the efforts of an important Harlem company and made it difficult for the group to command widespread support for its continuance when foundation funds were cut off. While addressing their plays to Black audiences, the Krigwa Players reserved a warm welcome "for all artists of all races and for all sympathetic comers and for all beautiful ideas."[4]

While DuBois was encouraging playwriting and sponsoring productions of Black plays for Black audiences, he and others were also concerned about both the content and the form of presentation of the nascent Afro-American theatre they were strenuously promoting. As early as 1916 DuBois had observed, in a statement prophetic of the current fascination with ritual as an appropriate model for Afro-American dramatic form, that

[3]"Krigwa Players' Little Negro Theatre." *The Crisis,* vol. 32, no. 3 (July, 1926), pp. 134-36.
[4]Playbill for Krigwa Players' first season in Harlem, New York, May, 1926.

throughout Africa "pageantry and dramatic recital are closely mingled with religious rites and in America the 'Shout' of the Church revival is in its essentials pure drama."[5] Another perceptive theorist and spokesman for the Black theatre movement of the time was Alain Locke, then professor of philosophy at Howard University and renowned today for his intellectual leadership. Exemplary of the quality of that leadership is his anthology, *The New Negro*, which not only includes much of the finest literary work of the Harlem Renaissance but which also attempts to analyze the aesthetic direction of the period.

Others had written disparagingly of the image of the Black performer as a song-and-dance comedian on the professional stage, but Locke saw hidden resources in the folk arts of Negro song, dance, and pantomime which could be exploited and transposed to the serious stage to provide what he called a "galvanizing stimulus." He called for Negro dramatic art to be liberated from the handicaps of both external disparagement and self-imposed limitations. He saw the need for experimentation in form and urged on Black theatre artists the courage to be original, to break with established dramatic convention of all sorts and develop their own idiom. Training and direction were indeed essential for Black artists, he maintained, but along the lines of their own instinctive patterns and idioms of expression, not superimposed from an alien source. Finally, Locke reaffirmed the importance of the African continuum in the arts of Afro-Americans. "One can scarcely think of a complete development of Negro dramatic art," he wrote, "without some significant artistic re-expression of African life and the traditions associated with it."[6] Continuing in this vein, he added these inspiring sentiments:

> If, as seems already apparent, the sophisticated race sense of the Negro should lead back over the trail of the group tradition to an interest in things African, the natural affinities of the material and the art will complete the circuit and they will most electrically combine.... Here both the Negro actor and dramatist can move freely in a world of elemental beauty, with all the decorative elements that a poetical emotional temperament could wish.[7]

[5]"Drama Among Black Folk." *The Crisis*, XII (August, 1916), p. 169.
[6]"The Negro and the American Stage." *Theatre Arts Monthly*, vol. X (February, 1926), p. 119.
[7]*Ibid.*

Central to the debate over the function and structure of Black theatre, then as now, is the prevailing view that the theatre of Black Americans should by definition be distinct from that of White America. The argument goes as follows. The two societies identified by the federal government's 1968 Kerner Report have, through their widely contrasting experiences, arrived at different conceptions of reality that seem to demand differing modes of creative expression. Black theatre that appears to be analogous in form to the established Euro-American theater is, therefore, deemed to be a thoughtless imitation of an alien culture and a betrayal of the true heritage of the race.

Addison Gayle, Jr., one of the more vocal proponents of the Black aesthetic, in the January/February 1977 issue of *First World* pinpoints the challenge confronting the Black artist who lives in a society where the very terms of existence are, in Mr. Gayle's words, defined by persons and forces antithetical to his being. The Black artist must "hold on to his own sense of reality," affirms Gayle, "while vigorously denying that offered by the society." The argument is developed along these lines:

> For him, the overwhelming question is whether or not the reality of the oppressed and the oppressor are fundamentally the same; or whether the rigors of living in a tyrannical society do not force upon the oppressed experiences, perceptions, and ways of viewing man and the world that are contradictory to that of those who are not oppressed. ... The refusal to accept white American definitions of reality leads to a refusal to accept its definitions of such concepts as manhood, heroism, beauty, freedom, and humanism.[8]

If such concepts are in fact defined differently by Black people and White, it follows that theatre as an art form involved in expressing these concepts will likewise be different for the two societies.

It is here that theatre as an industry that must be financially viable if it is to function becomes a crucial issue. White American theatre represents the dominant culture. This cultural dominance is sustained not alone through numerical superiority or an unbroken Euro-American tradition, but in practical terms through economic control of the means of theatrical production. Profes-

---

[8]"Blueprint for Black Criticism." *First World,* Vol. 1, No. 1 (January/February, 1977), pp. 41-45.

sional theatre in America is and always has been in White hands. Even the so-called independent Black professional companies that exist today are dependent on regular handouts from White philanthropic foundations. Withdrawal of these grants is financially crippling and leads to almost certain demise.

In the past Blacks have sought to join the mainstream professional theatre to which they were first denied access, then grudgingly admitted, and finally allowed entrance on terms that perpetuated their image as song-and-dance clowns performing for the amusement of White audiences. Little wonder that the musical comedy theatre, generally conceded to be America's gift to the world stage, fell into disrepute among the very Blacks who had provided its genesis and contributed to some of its brightest days. Occasionally, nowadays, Black artists appear on Broadway in serious productions that offer some thoughtful insights into Black life and history; other actors go there to practice their craft on the rare occasions when they are tapped for a challenging role from the world theatre. In the main, however, those Black artists who remain on Broadway are in the business of entertainment, and while art and entertainment are not necessarily incompatible, the art of Black theatre on Broadway is unlikely to be fundamentally different from the established formulas and standards that apply to the Euro-American theatre and will continue to seem a weak echo of the dominant culture.

The fact is that Broadway is the wrong marketplace for the theatre experimentalist, Black or White. But whereas experiments in White theatre are departures from the norm and properly find a home on the fringes of Broadway or in community-supported regional theatres, Black experimental theatre is (or should be) the norm for Black artists, for all Black theatre that is not simply imitative is in the process of becoming and deserves an assured place in the cultural life of the nation. This is a condition that too few of the major drama critics are willing to concede, and, as a result, most critical response exhibits an intolerance of Black theatre productions that do not fall within readily categorized modes.

The task of forging a new Black theatre that would express in meaningful ways the true voice and vision of Afro-Americans cannot be carried out on Broadway. That is why practitioners of serious Black theatre have found it necessary, time and again, to turn to Black communities for sustenance and support. How have these communities responded to efforts to locate dramatic theatres in their midst? Recent years have witnessed a significant improvement in audience turnout to Black shows, but overall the record of support for community-based theatres remains discouraging. In Harlem alone, that metropolis of Black artistic talent, some eighteen or twenty attempts have been made in the last half-century to establish a strong resident theatre organization. All have failed. Few Harlem theatres exist today; none can claim to be flourishing.

The reasons for this continuing lack of support for the Black community theatre are easily adduced. Blame has been laid on the type of plays produced, which are too narrowly focused on polemical and political views not always shared by the community. Plays that uplift the mind and enrich the spirit are rarely seen. Paucity of entertainment, in the best sense of the word, has also been remarked. The Black urban community, plagued by high unemployment and economic depression, is not financially able to maintain a community theatre. The location and atmosphere of the theatre buildings have been criticized as uninviting if not downright forbidding. The lack of a theatregoing tradition among Blacks has also received its share of reproach. There is a modicum of truth in all these complaints, as well as in the fact that the Black press, despite an enviable record in defense of Black causes, has not always been as supportive of Black theatre as the need required.

In 1953 Miles Jefferson, theatre reviewer for the Atlanta University journal *Phylon,* complained that no Black newspaper or periodical in the Manhattan area carried a regular theatre column on Blacks in professional theatre written by a Black critic. His profferred services had been turned down on the excuse that readers of Manhattan's Black papers were not interested in the Broadway theatre. Commented Mr. Jefferson: "How may one appreciate and enjoy any art if he is not enlightened concerning it? And how may he be exposed to it better than through the Negro Press?"[9] Happily, the situation in recent times has changed for the better, but a tradition of theatregoing (or, preferably, theatre participation) is not instantly created; it is developed over years of exposure to the practice of theatre and to illuminating

[9]"The Negro on Broadway, 1952-53." *Phylon,* Vol. 14, No. 3 (1953), pp. 268-279.

commentary on theatrical performance. It will take time before Black theatres reap the benefit of a more enlightened editorial policy by the press regarding theatre reviews.

The question of how to encourage and protect needed experimentation in the Afro-American theatre while retaining and expanding audiences who have been nurtured on standard theatre fare is the knottiest of all problems faced by responsible Black theatre practitioners. Most of them, concerned as much with survival as with aesthetic considerations, tend to adopt a pragmatic approach of using whatever form seems to work best for a particular production and are content to bequeath the search for a recognizable Afro-American theatre form to the pens of critics and theorists. Some others have turned away altogether from the staging of static texts on a conventional stage in favor of a type of participatory theatre by players and audience in a shared space of interaction and celebration.

This kind of eclecticism is not necessarily wasteful or self-indulgent. A variety of approaches is desirable in order that honest experimentation may be carried out over a broad spectrum and provided that such efforts are scrutinized in the searching light of informed criticism and public appraisal. It should be stated, however, that serious experimental theatre cannot be successfully pursued on a part-time schedule, or by inadequately trained artists, or without appropriate and flexible plant and equipment. All of which brings us back to the question of money. The dilemma was evident to Theophilus Lewis, drama critic of *The Messenger* in the 1920s: "Without economic autonomy, the Negro stage can never become the flexible medium for the expression of the spirit of Negro people it ought to be."[10] Lewis was among the first of many writers to call for the founding of a permanent national Black theatre where the work of developing a theatrical identity for Afro-Americans could begin. He even went so far as to suggest that a monthly contribution from the five richest Black churches in New York City would enable a company to be formed that would be able to afford the services of the most talented artists.

Of all the expressions of Black theatre needs down through the

[10]Quoted in "Theophilus Lewis and the Theatre of the Harlem Renaissance" by Theodore Kornweibel, Jr. *The Harlem Renaissance Remembered*, ed. Arna Bontemps (New York: Dodd, Mead & Co., 1972), pp. 171-89.

years, the call for a national Black theatre has been the most
persistent. Alain Locke emphasized the need early in the century
when he asked that native talent be cultivated beyond the demands and standards of the marketplace, and in the protected
housing of the art theatre where it could flower to the utmost
perfection. Every decade since that time has heard the appeal
repeated with growing insistence and has witnessed short-lived
attempts to establish such an institution. That the absence of a
national Black theatre is as keenly felt today as it was fifty and
more years ago is manifest in the view of Ernie McClintock,
respected leader of one of the more active and vigorous Harlem-
based groups, the Afro-American Studio Theatre founded in
1966. Writing in the *Black Alliance Newsletter* of February 1978
on the problems confronting the Black theatre movement at the
present time, McClintock cites first the lack of one major theatre
company that produces frequent quality productions and has
captured the imagination and support of large numbers of Blacks,
thereby setting a strong positive example for others. "Examples
of artistic excellence in theatre are crucial," he says; "an involved
and sincere effort to establish a true national Black theatre must
be realized immediately."

This writer readily acknowledges that a single prestigious company of talented Black theatre artists working in a national house
to explore, develop, and present the finest productions of Afro-
American theatre is a desired goal. But a national Black theatre
must be truly national. While training, research, experimentation, and skilled performance should proceed with a resident
company, including actors, dancers, musicians, singers, and other
types of entertainers, the national theatre should open its doors to
productions from other Black theatres, which should be invited
to present works there that are judged of value in helping to
create and define standards of beauty and excellence pertinent to
the Black experience. Conversely, productions of the national
company would tour other theatres in order to share its dis-
coveries and creations with the national Black community.

It cannot be a futile hope that America will one day build and
support a House of Black Culture, including a national Black
theatre, situated in one of the major Black cities. Such an edifice
should not be viewed as capitulation to a separatist ideology. On
the contrary, it would help to unite the two societies by giving,

for the first time, tangible recognition to the different cultural legacy of Afro-Americans, enabling them to approach the Euro-American culture as equals rather than as satellites. For in truth, Afro-Americans have contributed much from their culture to the greatness of America in the arts, as in other walks of life, and in return they have been left the poorer for their gifts. Elegant national and municipal cultural centers rise steadily around the country, all of them designed as symbols of the dominant White culture that, at best, is deemed tangential to the rich racial heritage of Black Americans. Amphitheatres are built for great symphonic summer festival productions that dramatize episodes from the saga of American history, but no open-air symphonic dramas of the Afro-American story are heard in the land. Instead, Black-controlled theatres, struggling ever for survival, occupy cramped basements and draughty lofts where gifted artists lurk around restively as if the shadows of slavery still hovered over their heads. In the revolutionary '60s the cry was: Black Theatre —Go Home! It is time now for Black theatre to come out of the shadows.

---

Throughout this book, the terms *Negro, Afro-American,* and *Black American* are used synonymously to refer to Americans of African descent. The word *Negro,* to which some opprobrium has lately been attached, is used only where historically appropriate.

I wish to acknowledge with gratitude the help of Mary Gould of the Drama Department at Dartmouth College in typing portions of the manuscript.

This book, Volume II of a two-part series on the Theater of Black Americans, covers "The Presenters: Companies of Players" and "The Participators: Audiences and Critics." Volume I deals with "Roots and Rituals: The Search for Identity" and "The Image Makers: Plays and Playwrights."

*The Presenters: Companies of Players*

# The Lafayette Players, 1917-1932

*by Sister M. Francesca Thompson, O.S.F.*

The original Lafayette Players was the first major professional Black dramatic company in America. Making a significant stride forward, this ambitious band of Black actors performed over a seventeen-year period from 1915 to 1932. They were successful in their attempt to step outside the confining mold that had been created for them by White writers, producers, and managers, and by both White and Black audiences since the early days of American theatre.

Up to the beginning of the present century, Blacks appeared on the stage primarily as caricatures of themselves. They were comic, shuffling misrepresentations of real-life people of color. The history of the minstrel show in America supports the view that, for many performers as well as for the majority of audiences, the Black man could be represented on the stage only in a manner conceived in some people's minds as an indolent, lazy-lipped buffoon with hankerchief-wrapped head. This outlandish "typical Negro" became, unhappily, the stock Negro character of the American theatre, despite the notable achievements of proud Black actors such as James Hewlett and Ira Aldridge.

Since 1900, however, the story of the progress of the Black man in the entertainment arts has been one of growing affirmation of manhood and full citizenship. Among the new breed of Black entertainers to come forward in the second decade of our century was Anita Bush. Miss Bush was a chorus member of the popular Williams and Walker musical comedy company, but she wished for an opportunity to do more than sing and dance. She conceived the idea of a Black dramatic stock company and although

"The Lafayette Players, 1917-1932" by Sister M. Francesca Thompson, O.S.F. This article appears for the first time in this volume and is printed here by permission of the author.

her idea was not entirely original, the method by which the company would function had been, prior to that time, unknown to Blacks.

As a girl growing up in Brooklyn, the daughter of a tailor whose clients were predominantly show-business people, Anita had come into contact with the theatre and had fallen hopelessly under its spell. Her first opportunity to act came when she and her sister were offered roles as extra serving-maids in a production of Shakespeare's *Antony and Cleopatra* presented at the Park Theatre in New York by a group of White professionals. Miss Bush says that she managed to be in every scene possible and learned everyone else's lines by heart. Her sister was in the production too and after dinner, over the dishpan, they would enact together the entire play line for line, alternating roles. "We felt certain," said Miss Bush, "that Broadway didn't know what talents it was missing." After this initial experience, she admits she was addicted for life and thereafter she and her sister played any part given to them when they could wheedle or implore the director, manager, or leading actors to hire them.[1]

At the age of sixteen and after much cajoling of her worried father, Anita was permitted to join the Williams and Walker company, then playing successfully in New York. She travelled to Europe with the group when it toured with the smash hit *In Dahomey* in 1903-1904, and she performed with them in London and throughout England and Scotland. She remained with the company after their triumphant return to New York. In 1909 George Walker was forced into retirement due to illness and the Williams and Walker company disbanded. Anita found herself without a job.

Undaunted by the temporary misfortune, Miss Bush chose four or five of the most talented chorus girls from the company and formed her own dancing group. They performed on the music-hall circuit for some years until a serious accident backstage in 1913 resulted in a critical back injury that kept Miss Bush on crutches for a year. Removal of the crutches was followed by a long fight with pneumonia. Confined to her bed for many weeks, Anita had time to rethink her earlier plans and to recon-

[1]Anita Bush, interview, New York, December 31, 1969. The author spent two days, December 31, 1969, and January 2, 1970, interviewing Miss Bush at the latter's home in New York.

struct her dream of a dramatic stock company. She vowed that on her recovery she would set out to fulfill her earlier ambition. There were at this time two Harlem theatres catering to colored patrons. The Lincoln Theatre was located at West 135th Street and The Lafayette Theatre at 132nd Street and Seventh Avenue. The latter boasted a Black comanager, Lester Walton. The Lincoln Theatre, a vaudeville house, had opened on Christmas Eve, 1908, as a store-front theatre with only 297 seats. Its proprietress, Mrs. Marie C. Downs, was considered by the Harlem community to be a very liberal White. In October 1915 she had the Lincoln renovated into more commodious quarters and. announced that the theatre had been built to give colored performers an opportunity to receive a hearing before the public. Mrs. Downs was assisted in the management of the theatre by Eugene Elmore who, because of his appearance, was usually referred to by theatre people as "Frenchy."

While still recuperating from her illness, Anita attended the Saturday matinee of a silent motion picture at the Lincoln. Due to a slump in vaudeville attractions, the house was being used for movies between bookings of live entertainment. Anita was strongly impressed with the attractiveness of the newly redecorated theatre and was distressed to see only six or seven persons enjoying the movie. She immediately decided to contact Frenchy about changing the face of the theatre. She told him that she wished to launch a new idea in New York theatrical circles: "a colored dramatic stock company called the Anita Bush Stock Company."[2] Speaking with a conviction that she didn't quite feel, she convinced Elmore that her group was already assembled and ready to go to work. She assured him, moreover, that she could guarantee him an eager and receptive crowd to fill his empty theatre.

Worried about the business slump that had hit the new theatre into which so much money had been invested, Elmore was evidently more than anxious to listen to any idea that might help to boost business. Anita says that he took to her plan so quickly that her head which was already spinning from fever felt even dizzier. For the first time she had spoken her dream aloud. Her positive, confident air impressed Elmore to such a degree that he did not stop to discuss money matters first, but asked how soon her company could be ready. Promising a finished produc-

[2]*Ibid.*

tion within two weeks, with a company ready to perform before his paying customers, pushing for a fair amount of money with which to pay her as yet nonexistent actors, Anita met Elmore the following Monday in the office of an attorney and signed a contract to legalize their verbal agreement.

Next Miss Bush contacted Billie Burke, a White director known around Harlem who had done some playwriting, and asked him to direct the company. The play chosen for the group's debut was one of Burke's own works, a light comedy titled *The Girl at the Fort.* Anita felt certain that she could find good character actors to fill the five required roles. She rushed around Harlem scouting for actors, knowing that Elmore wanted pictures taken as soon as possible for use in advertising the opening performance in the Black newspapers of New York. Miss Bush ran into an old friend, Jesse Shipp, a Black scenarist, vaudevillian and director of no little reputation who had worked on most of the Williams and Walker productions. When she told him of her plans, Shipp promptly assured her that she was crazy and that the time was not ripe for such a venture. He felt that there weren't enough Black actors proficient in straight drama to provide a competent cast. Undaunted by his negative reaction, Anita persevered with her search that was to yield a more than adequate cast for her initial production.

"Tab shows" were very much in vogue at this time as fillers between vaudeville acts or between the silent movies that were becoming more and more popular. These shows were short skits, usually musical, that ran from fifteen to twenty minutes. Charles Gilpin, who had made a name for himself at the famous Pekin Theatre in Chicago and who later would win renown as the creator of the lead role in Eugene O'Neill's *The Emperor Jones,* was engaged in such a "tab" act with a young woman. Gilpin was the first person whom Anita met after her encounter with Shipp. She explained her plans and he responded with interest saying, "You know, Bushy, I'd have to bust up my act...but then, we ain't doing nothing anyway."[3]

Next Miss Bush met Dooley Wilson, well-known Harlem musician and comedian who, years later, became celebrated for his supporting role in the film *Casablanca;* then Carlotta Freeman,

[3]*Ibid.*

who was delighted at the prospect of work; and finally, a handsome young man, very popular among Harlem theatrical folk, named Andrew Bishop. Bishop brought the number of Anita's company to a grand total of five. He was to remain with the group intermittently throughout the entire seventeen years of its existence and at a later date he would temporarily assume the role of manager and director.

Through newspaper articles, advertisements and pictures, the newly formed stock company was introduced to the Harlem community. Both popular Black newspapers in Harlem, the *New York Age* and the *New York Amsterdam News*, heralded the grand opening of the company at the New Lincoln Theatre on November 15, 1915. *The Girl at the Fort*, a farcical comedy, was very well received by both the public and the press, with reviewers applauding the pioneer efforts at legitimate drama by a Black company. The *Amsterdam News* of November 19, 1915, found the show to be "exhilarating, vitalizing, and charming as well."

The company played successfully for six continuous weeks at the New Lincoln Theatre, changing the bill several times during its engagement. During this time Billie Burke assumed the managerial as well as directorial duties for the company, since Elmore had moved to the rival theatre, the Lafayette. Burke allowed Miss Bush to select the company's repertoire of plays. Most of the casts, like the one for *The Girl at the Fort*, were of necessity small.

Anita Bush's Stock Company met with such success, in those first weeks of trial, that the business-minded proprietress, Marie Downs, requested that Miss Bush change the name of her group to the "Lincoln Players." The request was promptly and firmly denied. Moreover, Miss Bush, taking advantage of the lenient contract between them, gave the theatre managers two weeks' notice and transferred her company to the rival Lafayette Theatre under Elmore. The newspapers announced that on December 27, 1915, the Anita Bush Stock Company would make its debut at the Lafayette Theatre in a new play called *Across the Footlights*.[4]

It must be admitted at this point that the group was far from an accomplished, sophisticated, or polished theatre company by today's standards. The players were still groping in the dark in

[4]Unidentified newspaper article in Anita Bush scrapbook. The omission of a playwright's name indicates that such information was not available.

many ways. Yet they accomplished more than to provide light entertainment for Black patrons. They afforded an education from the stage for participants as well as audiences. Members of this pioneer group were forerunners of a new generation of Black performers and were recognized as such by an equally new kind of Black audience. True, no Black playwrights were being heard through these actors. Angry voices of protest against "the system" did not echo from the stage of the Lincoln or Lafayette Theatres. The particular contribution of this company consisted of training the Black actor by providing opportunities for him to appear in a variety of acceptable dramatic roles. An understanding of and appreciation for this new form of entertainment did not develop among Black audiences overnight. Both audience and performers needed time to be reeducated and thanks to Anita Bush and her neophyte company, school-time had begun.

When he was questioned about the aims and ambitions of the early members of the Lafayette Players, the revered actor Clarence Muse, then 86 years old, who joined the group in 1916 and became one of its brightest stars, said reflectively:

> Our aim was to give vent to our talent and to prove to everybody who was willing to look, to watch, to listen, that we were as good at drama as anybody else had been or could be. The door was opened a tiny bit to us and, as always, the Black man when faced with an open door, no matter how small the wedge might be, eased in.[5]

The audiences that the company had delighted at the New Lincoln followed the players when they transferred to the Lafayette. The Black drama critic for the *New York Age*, Lester Walton, was also comanager of the Lafayette Theatre, a connection that certainly added to the company's ability to generate good newspaper reviews of their performances. Yet Walton was no mere puff-writer. In welcoming the company's first production at the Lafayette, in an article dated December 30, 1915, he declared that while the Stock Company might not reach the peak of greatness in its time it would be remembered "as having introduced to New York an IDEA which was bound to take deep root, to spread,

[5]Clarence Muse, interview, Perris, California, August 23, 1969. The author spent one week, August 23-29, 1969, interviewing Mr. Muse at his home in Perris, California. In succeeding footnotes, the initial date, August 23, will be used to designate the week's interview.

and to rebound to the good of the Negro on the stage." Mr. Walton described the company's work as a "great and meritorious effort being made to raise the standard of the colored theatrical profession; and an endeavor to prove that the Negro can do other than sing and dance, an endeavor that warrants the hearty support and cooperation of all members of our race."

At the Lafayette, the company presented a new play every week. Their second offering, on January 3, 1916, was an adaptation titled *The Gambler's Sweetheart* which was based on a popular Broadway hit, *The Girl of the Golden West* by David Belasco. A few days later it was announced that the next play would be a condensed version of Boucicault's drama, *The Octoroon,* that treated the controversial question of race relations in the southern United States. The choice of this play was directly influenced by criticism that was being voiced against the company for neglecting plays dealing with Negro life. The production called for seven additional actors and among new members joining the company, who remained with the group for some time, were J. Francis Mores, a baritone singer, and Mrs. Charles Anderson, who later assumed her own name, Ida Anderson, after some success in the theatre. Following this production, other new names constantly appeared in the cast lists. On January 16, 1916, the *New York Age* announced that Miss Bush was offering a prize for the best 60-minute sketch dealing with Negro life, but there is no indication that this offer produced any scripts that were subsequently presented by the company.

An advertisement in the *New York Age* of March 2, 1916, stated that Charles Gilpin would star in a forthcoming production, *Southern Life,* directed by A. C. Winn, and that Mr. Gilpin would be supported by "The Lafayette Stock Company." This was the first time that the new name of the company appeared in print. It is also the first indication that the company had a new director in the person of Mr. Winn. Although there were to be several names attached to the group in ensuing years, they considered themselves from this time forth to be the Lafayette Players. Apparently, Anita Bush was no longer adamant about her name being used because in spite of the changed name, Miss Bush remained with the Players until 1920, not leaving them until opportunity to begin another new venture was afforded her.

When in 1916 Lester Walton temporarily surrendered the management of the company, it was bought out by the Elite Amusement Corporation, a theatrical agency that aimed to control a circuit of theatres for colored patrons throughout the country. The Players were then known as the Elite Amusement Company; later when management rights were purchased by the Quality Amusement Corporation the company acquired that name also. The new owner was Robert Levy, a man whose association with the Lafayette Players continued to the end and whose influence was considerable. He brought in the best directors, A. C. Winn and Edgar Forrest, and is reported to have said of the Players: "They have a special gift for this art of acting. Blacks are not synthetic but actors who are soul-feeling."[6]

The success that had attended the initial efforts of the Players at the Lincoln Theatre continued unabated at the Lafayette. Their offerings changed weekly and their repertory ranged from drama to farce with an occasional musical. Many of the plays they presented were well-known Broadway successes by popular playwrights of the time, such as Augustus Thomas and George Broadhurst. In March, 1916, they offered a play titled *For His Daughter's Honor,* billed as a four-act race play with Gilpin starring. Later that month *Within the Law,* a recent Broadway hit by Bayard Veiller, was so popular that the company had to perform twice daily at 2:15 P.M. and 8:15 P.M. in order to accommodate the crowds. According to manager Elmore, the fame of the Lafayette Players at this time had spread so far that on a certain Saturday night some 1,500 people had to be turned away, many of them having come from Philadelphia to attend a performance.[7]

With such a rigorous production schedule to meet, the Players must have worked without respite. Since the law prohibited dramatic performances on Sundays, it was the day off for the company when the house ran either vaudeville acts or the popular silent movies. According to Clarence Muse, rehearsals were held every weekday after matinee performances. One can assume that Sundays were also used for extended rehearsals. On Thursday, parts for next week's show were handed out. Actors were assigned

[6]Clarence Muse interview, August 23, 1969.
[7]*Indianapolis Freeman,* April 1, 1916.

their roles and their moves were roughed out. Lines had to be learned in two days. Because of the short rehearsal time, a great deal of improvisation occurred at performance. As Muse put it: "The ability to think fast on your feet was what determined if you were quality, and your salary depended upon your quality."[8] Admission prices in 1916 were kept low: 5 and 10 cents for matinee performances, 10, 15 and 25 cents for evenings.

There arose some financial difficulties and due to disagreement between Lester Walton and the owners of the theatre, Walton left the Lafayette as comanager. In February, 1916, he had published an article on the financial state of the operation. The landlord, he indicated, asked $25,000 annual rent for the building; between May, 1914, and February, 1916, Walton had spent over $15,000 for house help, all of it colored. The Players company had received over $1,000 in three weeks, with $300 still due to them. Walton did not know that within a few years he would be returning to the Lafayette as sole manager. Always a man who looked to the future and prodded members of his race ever upward and forward, he remained a staunch supporter of the Lafayette Players and followed closely their career in his weekly columns in the *New York Age*. This paper continued to announce each new show and to review the current week's offering. From 1915 through 1923, every issue of the *Age* carried one or more articles concerning the Lafayette Players.

When Charles Gilpin quit the company in 1916 because of dissatisfaction with the salary offered by the new management, Clarence Muse was lured away from the Lincoln tab shows to replace Gilpin at a weekly salary of $90. Muse made his first starring performance with the Players in Harlem in their production of *The Master Mind*. His association with the company continued periodically until the Lafayette Players finally disbanded. As Muse recalls his initiation, he says that he felt out of place as an "Ethiopian" among all of the other "high-yellow Negroes" in the company.[9] He is a well-built man of dark complexion and pronounced features. Muse decided to change his appearance on stage by skillful use of white make-up and a blonde wig constructed especially for him by a German wig-maker. Muse re-

[8]Clarence Muse interview, August 23, 1969.
[9]*Ibid.*

flects in amusement that the alteration served no real purpose except as an ego booster for himself. He recalls that before his first entrance on stage he was required to speak lines off-stage. The audience, well acquainted with his voice, sat waiting for him to appear. They were not prepared for the white Muse who entered and it often took several minutes for them to cease clapping and stamping their feet in appreciation of the excellent make-up job which he had executed.

While the Lafayette Players themselves never produced Shakespeare, their success in legitimate theatre in Harlem probably influenced the production of *Othello* by Edward Sterling Wright at the Lafayette Theatre in May, 1916, as a contribution to the tercentenary celebrations of Shakespeare's death. Subsequently in 1923 the theatre was host to productions of *The Comedy of Errors* and *The Taming of the Shrew* by the Ethiopian Players of Chicago. Among notable revivals mounted by the Players in their early years were *The Count of Monte Cristo, The Three Musketeers,* and *Camille* by Alexander Dumas; Goethe's *Faust* with songs incorporated from the operatic version of the play; Moliere's *The Follies of Scapin,* and others. *Madam X* by Alexander Brisson, one of their most ambitious productions, was outstandingly successful and featured Abbie Mitchell in the leading role. Her performance was so well received that it invited comparison with the notable actress Sarah Bernhardt. Once again the Players were proving that they were not willing to limit themselves to what had previously been prescribed as material suitable for Black performers.

In April, 1916, Anita Bush was asked to come to Chicago to start a new group of Lafayette Players under the direction of Edgar Forrest. It was not to be a rival company but rather an extension of the New York group. Invited by the managers of the Grand Theatre in Chicago to come and pump new life into a waning theatrical house, Anita gladly accepted this new challenge. The second company was born and then, in May of the same year, to answer the growing demand for the Lafayette Players to perform in the eastern cities of Washington and Baltimore, a third group of Players was formed. By the end of 1917 there was one group of Players at the home theatre in Harlem and two travelling companies on the road. The *New York Age*, the *New York Amsterdam News*, the *Chicago Defender*, the *Indianapolis Freeman*, and the *Pittsburgh Courier* all carried reviews of the Players' productions. A great deal of space was devoted to their activities by the *Indianapolis Freeman* not only because the editor, George L. Knox, was particularly fond of the theatre but also probably because in 1917 his grandson, Edward Thompson, had joined the Lafayette Players.

By August, 1918, advertisements for the Lafayette productions stated in bold letters: "Lafayette Theatre: The House of Quality — The Home of Class." From 1918 until their demise in 1932, the Players sought to deserve that accolade. They performed almost continuously, and frequent newspaper articles chronicle their activities and achievements during these years. Their appearances on the travelling circuits are faithfully recorded by the Black newspapers that continued to support their work. Between 1926 and 1928 there appears to be a waning of public interest in the group, reflected in the occasional references to their productions in the major newspapers.

When the financial slump hit this country in the late twenties, the Lafayette Players were among the first to be affected by a general decline in show business. In 1928, therefore, Robert Levy once again purchased the right to their management and announced their move from New York as a home base to the newly built Lincoln Theatre in Los Angeles, California. Interest in the Players was renewed as they presented revivals of many of their former favorite attractions that had brought them such popularity on the East Coast and during their touring engagements.

Opening with a production of *Rain,* which had met with so much success on Broadway when it starred Jeanne Eagles, the Lafayette production starred Evelyn Preer. The Players ran for over fifty-four consecutive weeks at the Los Angeles Lincoln Theatre and played to mixed audiences which were largely composed of members of the Hollywood set. During this time Clarence Muse, who was producing his own musical show for nightclub patrons, was persuaded to rejoin the Players and recreate one of his most famous roles, that of Dr. Jekyll and Mr. Hyde.

Muse and Evelyn Preer also did a successful production of Dubose Heywood's famed drama *Porgy*. In addition, the Players added to their old repertoire such new productions as *Anna Christie*, *Desire Under the Elms*, *What Price Glory*, and *Irene*. By 1932, however, the curtain was lowered for the last time. Many factors, not the least of which was financial, caused the Lafayette Players finally to disband. Harry Levette wrote the obituary notice in his July 23, 1932 column for the *Chicago Defender:*

> After a noble experiment both on the part of the Lafayette Players and Jules Wolf, manager-director of the Lincoln Theatre, the notable company closed last Sunday night [July 17]. Their future plans are not known at present. There is no doubt that the present scarcity of money and the necessity for everyone parceling out their amusement budget was the cause that prevented a successful return. In 1928 when the Players first came to the Coast money was plentiful and for forty-two weeks there were nightly waiting lines, a large percentage of the audience being white. ... It is greatly to be regretted...but drama could not be made a go, but there is this consolation...in the fact that nothing is a go now, unless it is the cheapest form of picture entertainment. ... All their work and that of the new members added here was of the highest artistry as in the past.

The Players were laid to final rest. They must have been aware of the irony in the fact that the same article that announced the company's closing also informed the public that the feature motion picture opening at the Lincoln Theatre on the following Sunday was to be a new all-colored film entitled *Harlem Is Heaven*. For so many productive years, Harlem had been almost that for the Lafayette Players.

The Lafayette Players had a profound influence upon Black American theatre history. Despite the handicaps of exploitation and mismanagement, existing sociological problems and public apathy, they persevered in their determination to perform the legitimate drama. They were thus responsible for helping to raise the standards of Black entertainment.

Except for the African Grove Theatre venture in 1820, no other Black theatre companies had attempted to concentrate on producing legitimate drama before the appearance of the

Lafayette Players in New York. Prior to the advent of the Players, there were no Black actors performing significant roles on Broadway. Charles Gilpin was the first Black actor to break the barrier and to receive serious attention from Broadway critics and audiences. In Hollywood, the Black performer was equated with the Black comic stereotype. This erroneous labeling was belied by the types of performances given by the Lafayette Players who were acclaimed by many Hollywood personages as well as by others associated with the theatre.

Spanning a period of seventeen years of almost uninterrupted and successful performances, the Players laid a foundation upon which the accomplishments of Black entertainers in today's American theatre have been built. As Alain Locke notes in his essay, "The Negro and the American Stage," the dramas of their time were essentially "anemic," deficient in the vital symbols and ideas to which Black audiences could relate.[10] However, the Lafayette Players brought to that drama, if not the gift of a Black tradition, the gift of a particular temperament and talent. Frequently, Blacks have been rated as "natural-born actors," without any real conception of what that designation, if true, actually means. Disparagingly, it could mean a recognition of the Black man's restriction to the interpretative, as distinct from the creative, aspect of drama; it could indicate a confinement, in terms of a second order of talent. It could mean a reducing of his talent to that of a mere mimic.

Locke reminds his readers that a comprehending mind realizes that the very life of drama is in dramatic instinct and emotion, and that true drama begins and ends in imitation. In a sense, the Lafayette Players were merely modeling themselves upon what White performers were doing, but even in their imitation a kind of liberation was expressed. They broke with a well-established tradition with which the Black performer had been previously associated. They proved that Black performers could work effectively and successfully in a dignified medium, a medium that, until the time of the Lafayette Players, had been closed to Black performers.

Due in great part to the work of the Players, existing barriers

[10]Alain Locke, "The Negro and the American Stage," *Theatre Arts*, X (February, 1926), p. 112.

to accepting Blacks in legitimate drama were broken down. By 1932 the Black performer, in various areas of theatre entertainment, had worked his way up through minstrelsy and the musical comedy shows to become a maker of songs and dances and a legitimate dramatic artist. In their seventeen years of existence, the Lafayette Players witnessed the emergence of the Black performer from the restricted Negro theatre of Harlem to a recognized place on the legitimate stage of New York, the theatre capital of the country.[11]

The Lafayette Players cannot be denied their importance as a part of this development. From 1915 to 1932 the Players contributed to the forward thrust given the Black performer in the entertainment world. They worked with whatever was at hand and within the restrictions placed upon them by the existing social climate. Clarence Muse described the early group as "performers who wished to perform for the sheer joy of giving vent to artistic expression." No matter what the psychological or sociological Black-White implications of the time, the Lafayette Players did succeed in expressing their creative selves. As their progress in the theatre is traced, it can be clearly noted that the Players advanced steadily in certain areas. They gained in experience and technique. Unfortunately the Black writer did not keep pace. It would have benefited both actors and writers if the progress made by the actors had been paralleled by a similar progress among Black playwrights.

True it is, as Alain Locke stated, that the art of the Black actor would have to seek, more and more, for materials in the "rich native soil of Negro life" rather than in the threadbare traditions of the White stage. In the years during which the Lafayette Players worked, it must be realistically admitted, a dearth of such material was available. In using what was readily at hand, the Players encouraged the creation of additional suitable materials. They were heralds of a time when the Black writer would be accepted among his White peers. New and startling Black dramas would be written after the Players' demise, but one may speculate how soon the writing of these dramas would have been possible had it not been for the endeavors of groups like the Lafayette

[11]James Weldon Johnson, *Black Manhattan* (New York: Atheneum, 1968), p. 224.

Players. Dramatic maturity is never sudden. Usually, as in nature, there is a period of seed nurturing before there can be a full flowering.[12] The Lafayette Players were a part of that period of maturation. The Black actor was accepted seriously as an important force in the American theatre at the end of the Lafayette Players' existence, rather than at their beginning. In 1926, at the conclusion of his association with members of the Players, David Belasco, one of the country's great directors, predicted that the Black artist would receive in the future more serious consideration than he had received in the past.[13]

For a theatrical group to be in existence for seventeen years is in itself a remarkable feat, considering the difficulty of maintaining a stable performing company. For this period of time, the Lafayette Players managed to retain a membership large enough and talented enough to earn for the group national attention and respect. Beginning in New York, they soon moved out into other parts of the country. They were responsible for the introduction of legitimate theatre to Black audiences in many states, and in more than twenty-five cities Black audiences saw, for the first time, Black entertainers performing in a medium that differed greatly from the usual minstrel-type comedy with which audiences were familiar. This fact is especially true in the southern cities where Blacks were allowed to attend theatres for the first time, and in cities like Baltimore where unsegregated seating was finally permitted.[14]

So unaccustomed were some of these novice audiences to serious dramatic entertainment that, on at least one occasion preceding a play in an Atlanta theatre, the manager had to instruct the audience on what to expect and how to behave during the performance.[15] Thus, the Players became educators as well as entertainers. They were instrumental in guiding their audiences to accept a more sophisticated and an intellectually superior form of entertainment. Especially advantageous to their audience was the fact that the Black performers, because of a greater understanding, were more patient with the occasional disruptions caused by

[12]Locke, "The Negro and the American Stage."

[13]David Belasco, "Tomorrow's Stage and the Negro," *Liberty,* IV (August 7, 1926), pp. 18-23.

[14]*New York Age,* Aug. 10, 1916, p. 6.

[15]Lincoln Perry, interview, Indianapolis, Indiana, April 12, 1970.

those who came to see them. Because of a lack of previous exposure to drama, Black theatregoers were not prepared to enjoy or to appreciate properly what was being presented to them for the first time. Many skeptical Blacks were taught by the Lafayette Players that legitimate drama was good entertainment.[16]

Appearing in more than two hundred and fifty plays, the Lafayette Players performed in productions never before, nor since, presented by an entirely Black company of actors. They were thus instrumental in educating White audiences to an awareness that Blacks did possess dramatic talent and were capable of serious dramatic portrayals. By acquainting Black audiences with legitimate theatre and by proving to White audiences that Black actors could successfully perform in serious drama, the Lafayette Players helped pave the way for other Black dramatic groups who were encouraged by their success. A few of the most important of these were the Negro Art Theatre, the Rose McClendon Players, the Alhambra Theatre, the Gilpin Players, and the WPA Federal Negro Theatre Project. Each of these groups included members who had originally been with the Lafayette Players.

The Players were to serve as an incentive to Black businessmen who began to venture into theatre management and theatre ownership. Prime examples of those who were encouraged in this manner were the already-named Lester Walton, and E. C. Brown and Andrew F. Stevens, Black Philadelphia bankers who eventually purchased the Lafayette Theatre.[17] The Players also gave rise to a new form of journalistic writing in the Black newspapers of the day. The *New York Age, New York Amsterdam News, Chicago Defender, Indianapolis Freeman, Pittsburgh Courier,* and *California Eagle* were among the noteworthy Black newspapers that engaged writers to review dramatic productions given by the Players. A few of these journalists were to become nationally known to Black readers as critics deserving attention. Among these were Lester Walton of the *Age,* Salem Tutt Whitney of the *Defender,* and R. W. Thompson of the *Freeman.*

The Lafayette Players have been justly credited with helping to open the doors of Hollywood to Black actors. Evelyn Preer was an

[16]Clarence Muse, interview, Perris, California, August 23, 1969.
[17]Article from *Afro-American,* June 20, 1936, in Anita Bush scrapbook.

acknowledged pioneer who made it easier for actresses who followed her to be taken seriously and to be more readily accepted by White film producers and directors.[18] Several of the Players became well known in the theatrical world at large. A few were to leave lasting marks upon their profession. In every instance where a former member of the Lafayette Players succeeded elsewhere, credit was given to the Players for having afforded the performer an entrance into the theatre, and for having provided for the entertainer an opportunity to learn and to grow in craftsmanship. Among the best-known of the former Lafayette company were Andrew Bishop, Lawrence Chenault, Charles Gilpin, Clarence Muse, "Dooley" Wilson, Ida Anderson, Laura Bowman, Inez Clough, Cleo Desmond, Evelyn Ellis, and Evelyn Preer. In an article printed in the *Baltimore Afro-American* written in 1936, the Lafayette Players were lavishly praised for having given Black artists a chance to pioneer, and over fifty names of prominent Black entertainers were listed as having won much of their success and subsequent fame through their association with the Lafayette Players. Though this is an incomplete list, there are enough names to substantiate the claim that the Lafayette Players had served until their closing as a training school for an impressive number of Black performers.[19]

Despite advances, the Black actor in 1932 was still considered something of a novelty on the legitimate stage in America. He had not been totally welcomed in the capacity of serious dramatic actor. Obstacles still stood in his way, not the least of which was the "black actors' dilemma" described by Clarence Muse. There existed in the theatre two separate audiences with which the Black actor was forced to deal. There was the White audience with its preconceived notions about what it should see when observing Blacks on the stage, and there was the Black audience eager and waiting to see authentic elements of Black life portrayed on the stage. For the sake of pride, the Black performer desired to entertain his Black audiences, but the power of the White man's dollar also compelled his attention and helped to direct the course of his actions. Many of his ambitions remained submerged because of the dilemma faced in trying to satisfy two different audiences,

---

[18]*Pittsburgh Courier,* April 12, 1930, p. 6.

[19]Article from *Afro-American,* June 20, 1936, in Anita Bush scrapbook.

both of which possessed certain psychological expectations as well as the desire for entertainment and amusement.[20]

For a time, the Lafayette Players were able to gratify the Black audience's interest in serious theatre by imitating Broadway's White repertory. But the time came when the imitation could no longer satisfy Blacks who began more insistently to clamor for a drama of their very own. Progressive critics who wished Black theatre ventures to succeed complained that, although theatres owned and operated by Blacks and for Blacks existed in New York, Chicago, New Orleans, Jackson, Memphis, Atlanta, Columbus in Ohio, Jacksonville, Yazoo City in Mississippi, Baton Rouge and Plaquemine in Louisiana, and Los Angeles, all of these theatres seemed devoted to imitating the White man's stage and the White man's acting, instead of developing a drama uniquely and distinctly Black.[21] Similar complaints were to grow increasingly frequent. One of the reasons given for the declining popularity of the Lafayette Players at the Lincoln Theatre in Los Angeles was that the productions were too "White" in content and presentation.[22]

It is the contention of this writer that this dilemma of the Black actor was one of the principal causes for the closing of the Players. It was not possible to continue trying to please two such divergent audiences. The purpose for founding the group had not necessarily been to produce Black theatre but rather to perform legitimate drama solely for the sake of performing and to prove the capabilities of Black performers in a new medium. If there occurred a surge toward Black consciousness during this period, the Lafayette Players, as a group, were not a part of it. It is natural, then, that they would suffer the consequences: a decline of interest in their performances by the very Black audiences they helped to build and who had previously supported them.

Perhaps the most important single reason for the closing of the Players was the great depression that swept the United States. Salem Tutt Whitney, writing in the *Chicago Defender,* declared that there was a "general decline in show business" all over the

---

[20]Clarence Muse, *The Dilemma of the Negro Actor,* a privately printed pamphlet, 1934.

[21]Unidentified magazine article in Anita Bush scrapbook.

[22]*California Eagle,* Dec. 6, 1929, p. 7.

country and reported regretfully that "the bottom seems to have suddenly fallen out of Colored show business."[23] It was, however, all business that would be affected by the depression that rocked the economic foundation of the nation. As early as 1929, the southern route of the once-prosperous Theatre Owners Booking Association (T.O.B.A.) was almost completely closed. Memphis, Atlanta, Birmingham, New Orleans, and Nashville, all of which had experienced a boom in Black patronage for a considerable time, were suddenly reported to have dropped far behind their previous successes in attracting patrons to Black theatres.[24]

An article in the July 19, 1929 issue of the *California Eagle* listed many actors as "idle." The article was a reprint from a New York paper and reported that the closing of such popular Black shows as *Porgy* in London, *Blackbirds* in New York, and *Showboat* in Boston had evidently brought many familiar faces back to Harlem. The large number of unemployed Black actors was further increased by the closing of the popular Lincoln Theatre due to a lack of funds.[25] In February, 1931, the *Eagle* carried the bold headline: "Depression Hits Stage and Screen."[26] In the East, Philadelphia, Baltimore, and Newark had suffered from a shortage of business at theatre box offices, giving their managers much justifiable concern. From Washington it was reported that the once-popular Howard Theatre had had only a "fairly successful season." In New York, two more of the largest theatres, the Lafayette and the Alhambra, had borne the painful burden of insufficient funds and of a declining business.[27]

Salem T. Whitney suggested to his readers that one reason for the poor business in the theatrical world was that the very sophisticated quality of the entertainment offered by the large movie houses was less expensive than that of theatres trying to produce legitimate drama. He observed that buyers of any commodity were looking for places where the most and the best could be obtained for the least amount of money. Theatre patrons were seeking as much variety in entertainment as was possible.[28]

[23]*Chicago Defender,* July 27, 1929, p. 6.
[24]*Ibid.*
[25]*California Eagle,* July 19, 1929, p. 10.
[26]*California Eagle,* Feb. 13, 1931, p. 10.
[27]*Chicago Defender,* Dec. 17, 1932, p. 5.
[28]*Ibid.*

The entire theatrical field went into a staggering recession. This was a financial slump from which the Black theatre was not to revive fully until the opening of the WPA Federal Theatre Project in Harlem, when opportunity would again knock genially at the door of Black performers.[29]

It was a combination of factors, then, that finally brought about the demise of the group that had for so long kept alive Anita Bush's dream. The fact that they closed or the reasons for closing cannot, however, diminish what was accomplished by the Lafayette Players while they were still a vibrant, contributing source of entertainment for the Black audience who appreciated and supported them for seventeen years. What the Lafayette Players as artists gave to American theatre history cannot be taken from them, for their contribution does have value and worth. It was a positive contribution that permeated theatrical circles of the time. They effectively achieved what their initiator, Anita Bush, had set out to achieve: recognition as legitimate stage artists. She was their own Black Moses who endeavored to bring the Black performer out of a wilderness of neglect and ignorance to a place where he could stand on equal ground with his White peers. Anita Bush left her everlasting mark on the age by creating the Lafayette Players.

---

[29]Unidentified magazine article in Anita Bush scrapbook.

# The Role of Blacks
# in the Federal Theatre, 1935-1939

*by Ronald Ross*

Theatre in America was in serious trouble even before the economic collapse in 1929. Threatened with extinction in the 1920's by the burgeoning popularity of movies and radio, the theatre refused to alter its traditional thinking and practices. Instead of making itself available to greater numbers of people throughout the country, this institution remained rooted to its belief that New York City was synonymous with theatre. The standard theatrical practice of raising admissions scales whenever production costs lessened profits was also myopic; this procedure invariably reduced the number of individuals who were able to afford playgoing.[1] Then, too, the theatre's reluctance to send its troupes on tour to cities other than those located along the eastern seaboard further underlined the increasingly exclusive character of this activity.[2] In the battle for the cultural dollar, the theatre's patently non-democratic development worked against its own continued existence.

With the advent of the depression in 1929, the already tottering position of the theatre worsened considerably. Largely because of its status as a "luxury item," this industry was among

"The Role of Blacks in the Federal Theatre, 1935-1939" by Ronald Ross. From *Journal of Negro History*, Vol. LIX, No. 1 (January 1974), pp. 38-50. Reprinted by permission of The Association for the Study of Afro-American Life and History, Inc. and the author.

[1] The cost of attending a play was considerably more expensive than the price of admission to a movie house. The average theatre ticket cost $2.25, whereas only 25 cents gained a person entrance to a movie.

[2] There were exceptions to this general policy. On occasion, such cities as Chicago, San Francisco, Los Angeles, and Atlanta received visiting players from New York.

the first to feel the economic shockwaves, suffering staggering setbacks in the areas of production, employment, and patronage. As one theatre after another closed its doors in favor of renting to movie managers, the shortsightedness of previous thinking in this cultural field became painfully apparent. Employment, always marginal in this medium, dipped to abysmally low levels. A theatrical trade journal concluded, on the basis of a survey conducted in the winter of 1931, that there were 25,000 unemployed workers in its specialty, 3,000 of whom were black artists and craftsmen.[3] Patronage, the very lifeline of the theatre, disappeared as wealthy philanthropists "shifted their dwindling fortunes into more practical uses."[4] Shortly after such wholesale desertions, however, the federal government surfaced in this field with the most ambitious theatre program ever attempted—an undertaking which proved to be one of the most seminal developments in black theatre history.

The Federal Theatre Project (1935-1939) was designed to reverse the aristocratic posture of earlier theatrical operations in this country. That it reflected, therefore, the revolutionary character of the early New Deal program was not accidental. As Loften Mitchell explained it, "With Roosevelt's election, the country gave up nostalgic dreams and decided to make a complete change. Roosevelt brought a surge of hope to all America. This bold hope made its way into the theatre."[5]

Challenging theatre tradition in several ways, the Federal Theatre Project was particularly bold in its plan to make drama available to the masses for the first time. This democratic objective—a development singular in theatre history—was considered hazardous because of the widespread public antipathy toward this type of cultural entertainment. Unique also to the theatre was this project's ambition of providing employment opportunities not to handfuls of select players, as was practiced elsewhere with state-financed theatres, but to thousands of

---

[3] *Variety* magazine conducted this survey; the findings were reported by Able Green and Joe Laurie in *Show Biz* (New York: H. Holt and Company, 1953), p. 336.

[4] Ray Allen Billington, "Government and the Arts: The WPA Experience," *American Quarterly* 13 (Winter 1961): 468.

[5] Loften Mitchell, *Black Drama: The Story of the American Negro in the Theatre* (New York: Hawthorn, 1967), p. 96.

workless artists and craftsmen who had had at least some experience in the professional theatre.

The selection of Hallie Flanagan as the project's national director was still another indication of the revolutionary nature of this New Deal offshoot. This decision by Roosevelt and Harry Hopkins, the WPA director and a classmate of Miss Flanagan's at Grinnell College, was made in the face of considerable pressure that they appoint a representative of the commercial theatre to the top position. Both men were convinced, however, that the project should be headed by someone who had impressive credentials in the non-commercial theatre and also possessed a national perspective.[6]

Shortly after taking over the directorship of the Federal Theatre Project, Miss Flanagan addressed regional and state directors of the project at an organizational meeting held in Washington, D.C. in early October, 1935.

> The stage too must experiment—with ideas, with psychological relationship of men and women, with speech and rhythm forms, with dance and movement, with color and light—or it must and should become a museum product. In an age of terrific implications as to wealth and poverty, as to peace and war, as to the relation of an artist to all these forces, the theatre must grow up. The theatre must become conscious of the implications of the changing social order, or the changing social order will ignore, and rightly so, the implications of the theatre.[7]

Indeed revolutionary, this challenge issued by the project's national director signaled the beginning of a new kind of theatre in America: one that would not close its eyes to the bitter reality of the hard times facing most of the nation's population. The lot of the forgotten man, with whom the Roosevelt leadership had demonstrated considerable concern in its multiple New Deal programs, now also became a major concern of the Federal Theatre Project. As Miss Flanagan warned, "no person can work effectively in this theatre unless he cares increasingly about the

[6] Federal Theatre Project Papers, also known as the Hallie Flanagan Papers (Washington, D.C.: Archives of American Art, The Smithsonian Institution), hereafter cited as FTP Papers.

[7] Delivered October 8, 1935 (FTP Papers).

theme engaging science and industry today—that is, a better life for more people."[8]

At a total cost of 46 million dollars, the Federal Theatre Project was a bargain to taxpayers because of its broad concept of what constituted theatre; in comparison, the recently opened John F. Kennedy Center for the Performing Arts, a single edifice ostensibly constructed as a government showpiece in the nation's capital, cost the public a similar amount. The WPA project not only employed an average of 10,000 theatre workers annually, but it also attracted over 65,000,000 people from 40 states to a whole smorgasbord of theatrical productions. In addition to renting unused theatre houses across the country, this project took its theatre directly to the people. Hence schools, churches, parks, civic clubs, factories, hospitals, closed-off streets, and local radio stations all became backdrops for Federal Theatre activities. Moreover, it provided a myriad of theatre-related but non-productional services to thousands of American communities, including workshops for theatre apprentices and service bureaus for the collection and distribution of theatre materials.

Within the sprawling framework of its national program, the Federal Theatre established special ethnic theatre projects so that these groups would be able to do plays of their own literatures. The French theatre in Los Angeles; the German theatre in New York City; the Italian theatre in Massachusetts, New York City, and Los Angeles; and the Negro theatre in several cities were among the specially designed units.

Aside from being favored with their own production units because the project's national leadership was determined to contribute to the development of black theatre, blacks also shared fully in other project activities. Not only did they participate in the dramatic productions staged by the non-ethnic units, but they were an integral part of such diverse theatre operations as workshops for playwrights and technical craftsmen, research bureau services to communities, and project publications which included the *Federal Theatre Magazine*. That blacks would share center stage with other groups was portended even before the project officially began in 1935, since they were involved at all levels in the planning of this new theatre venture. In fact, it was during

[8] *Federal Theatre Magazine* 1 (March 1936): 14.

the project's organizational meetings that the famed Negro actress, Rose McClendon, first suggested that there be separate Negro units to insure the production of plays dramatizing black themes and exhibiting black talents.[9] Miss McClendon's suggestion that separate black theatre units be established was enthusiastically supported by the project's national leadership. The composition of the New York City project—the first project organized in the Federal Theatre— was an early indication that this government program would be one whose actual operation was as democratic as its rhetoric. Consequently, two of the four theatre units set up in New York in 1935 were the regular Federal Negro Theatre, housed in the Harlem community's Lafayette Theatre, and the Negro Youth Theatre, also located in the Lafayette but designed to develop inexperienced and lesser-known talents. In addition, New York was the setting for two Negro projects begun the following year: the African Dance Unit, composed of Nigerian troupers stranded in this country because of the Ethiopian crisis; and the Vaudeville Unit, stocked with veteran musical-comedy performers. These New York projects alone employed nearly one-thousand black theatre personnel, over half of whom were actors and directors.[10]

Aside from the New York units, the Federal Theatre sponsored Negro theatre projects which spanned the nation's entire landscape. Hartford, Boston, Salem, Newark, and Philadelphia in the East; Raleigh, Atlanta, Birmingham, and New Orleans in the South; Cleveland, Detroit, Peoria, and Chicago in the Midwest; and Seattle, Portland, and Los Angeles in the West joined New York as the initial centers of black drama. Additional units in San Francisco, Okmulgee (Oklahoma), Durham, Camden, and Buffalo started operations in 1936. By the project's conclusion, therefore, twenty-two American cities had served as headquarters for black theatre units.[11] Unquestionably, such dispersed ex-

[9] FTP Papers.

[10] J. F. McDougald, "The Federal Government and the Negro Theatre," *Opportunity* 14 (May 1936): 135-137.

[11] Regarding significant data on the organization of black units in the Federal Theatre Project, see Sterling A. Brown, "The Federal Theatre," in *Anthology of the American Negro in the Theatre*, ed. Lindsay Patterson (New York: Publishers Company, Inc., 1967), pp. 101-110; Edith Isaacs, *The Negro in the American Theatre* (New York: Theatre Arts, 1947); and FTP Papers.

posure was important not only to its black participants but also
to the black population in general because it previously had not
been allowed to surface in the national culture. As New Deal
historian William Leuchtenburg recently reminded, the Federal
Theatre pioneered in the promotion of ethnic diversity.

> What is much more to the point is the shocking degrees to which
> Negroes in the past were not permitted to be a visible part of the
> national culture. The New Deal began the process of change.[12]

Widespread exposure meant, moreover, that this government
theatre had an opportunity to accomplish something that it never
should have had to attempt in the first place—to dramatize to
white America the essential humanity of its black citizenry. Although it is highly unlikely that this objective was realized, the
great amount of favorable publicity attending the work done by
blacks throughout the project did reflect the general public's
acceptance of these minority members as worthy contributors to
the cultural life of the nation.[13]

Although the Federal Theatre was not able to erase the color
line completely, as Grace Overmeyer contended in *Government
and the Arts*,[14] it was effective enough so that it had less actual
discrimination than any other Roosevelt program. Behind this
record stood the fact that the theatre project, in contrast to New
Deal programs elsewhere, crusaded openly against minority discrimination. Its national director set the tone for this assault by
calling for a theatre that was free from racial prejudice.[15] To help
implement this conviction, Miss Flanagan directed her sub-
ordinates to enforce strictly the WPA prohibitions against prej-
udicial actions. Hence when a white project manager attempted
to segregate Negro actors and white technicians travelling to
Dallas in a private railroad car, the actors succeeded in their

[12]William Leuchtenburg, "The Great Depression and the New Deal," in
*Interpreting American History: Conversations with Historians*, Part 2, ed.
John A. Garraty (New York: The Macmillan Company, 1970), p. 190.

[13]According to Edith Isaacs in "National Theatre 1940," *Theatre Arts Monthly* 24 (January 1940): p. 58, the "most important contribution of the Federal
Theatre is the enormous amount of publicity it received."

[14]Grace Overmeyer, *Government and the Arts* (New York: W. W. Norton &
Company, 1939).

[15]Brown, "Federal Theatre," p. 101.

demand that the official be fired.[16] Then, too, the white assistant director of the entire vaudeville and circus program was removed from the project payroll because he was unable to work amicably with blacks.[17] As one theatre participant put it to the Dies Committee investigating the project in 1938, "those who were prejudiced found it extremely difficult to get along in the Federal Theatre."[18] Such a democratic posture proved unfortunate later on, however, when the same committee accepted the racially integrated project activities (including social affairs) as corrobative evidence of subversive activity because, in the words of Chairman Martin Dies of Texas, "racial equality forms a vital part of the Communistic teachings and practices."[19]

The theatre project's sensitivity to minorities also extended into the area of play selection. For example, the national leadership intervened to prevent the production of Octavus Ray Cohen's *Come Seven* by the Newark black unit because of widespread indignation by the Negro community over what they believed was an unseemly choice of play material. Leading the protests was the NAACP, whose Roy Wilkins likened the Cohen drama to the stereotyped theatrical fare usually served up by the Broadway stages. Wilkins further challenged the government project to "rise above these old habits of the American theatre."[20] In truth, the play was similar to an "Amos and Andy" farce, with the plot centered around a Negro who pawns his wife's diamond ring; and blacks were portrayed as monopolizing such activities as crap-shooting and chicken-stealing. Consequently, when the director of the project's National Play Bureau, Emmet Lavery, met with a delegation of protesting Negro leaders, he agreed to cancel *Come Seven,* explaining that there was more important material in the field which the project could use to advantage, and would not constitute, as did the Cohen

[16]FTP Papers.

[17]*Ibid.*

[18]U.S. Congress, Special House Committee on Un-American Activities, "Investigation of Un-American Propaganda Activities in the U.S.," Hearings, 75th Congress, 3rd Session, December 7, 1938, 4: 2857 (hereafter cited as "Dies Committee Hearings").

[19]*Ibid.,* p. 2858.

[20]Record Group 69, "Records of the Federal Theatre Project, Negro Drama File" (Washington, D.C.: National Archives).

play, a poor representation of an American ethnic group. Lavery cautioned, however, that the black unit in Newark—and not the national office—had selected the play in the first place.[21] Obviously the project's leadership was sensitive to what black playwright John Silvera, himself a participant in the Federal Theatre, called the nefarious role of drama in the perpetuation of racial stereotypes.[22] Although questionable in its sweeping assertion, Silvera's conclusion was valuable nonetheless because it called attention to the commercial theatre's responsibility in promoting accurate depictions of the nation's ethnic groups. The Federal Theatre, with its democratic concerns, challenged the aristocratic patterns long practiced by the Broadway stages.[23] In the process, this government project helped blacks to move one step closer to true emancipation—an emancipation at once social and economic as well as political.

Although unemployment has traditionally been commonplace in the theatre, there nevertheless has always existed a much higher rate of joblessness among black artists than among their white counterparts. One early victim of this pattern was Ira Aldridge (1804-1867), a Negro actor who was forced to abandon this country for Europe in order to secure the types of roles appropriate for an individual of such immense theatrical gifts. Once relocated in Europe, the talented Aldridge went on to become one of the truly legendary Shakespearean actors. More recently, Broadway stars Charles Gilpin and Rex Ingram discovered the added burden of seeking acting roles as black performers. What was particularly unsettling to Gilpin, the celebrated lead in *The Emperor Jones,* was the unavailability of parts written for black actors but performed by whites in blackface.[24]

Ingram, following several successful portrayals on the Broadway stages, suddenly found himself out of work in 1936. Jobless for two years, bankrupt, and dispossessed of all his belongings, he decided "to chuck everything and get on a tramp steamer for

[21]Telephone conversation with Emmet Lavery, November 20, 1971.

[22]John D. Silvera, "Still in Blackface," *Crisis* 46 (March 1939): 76.

[23]The challenge was tacit because the government had assured the commercial theatre that it would not interfere with its operations or purposes.

[24]Quoted by Mary B. Mullet in "Where Do I Go from Here?" *American Mercury* 41 (June 1921): 55.

the horizon."[25] It was at this low point in Ingram's career that the Federal Theatre rescued him, offering the Henri Christophe role in William DuBois's *Haiti* (1938) to the Negro star.[26]

The WPA theatre project was a godsend to thousands of other black artists as well because it presented them with their first opportunity to participate fully in the field of professional drama. In the process, it challenged a couple of extremely facile contentions which had long burdened the black actor and black community alike. The first idea was the notion that Negroes were "natural actors" who did not require any apprenticeship. As Edith Isaacs stressed, there is generally no remark "that is so disparaging to the Negro actor, singer, musician, as the one— often intended as a high compliment—that he is a natural born actor, who does not benefit by training."[27] Why this belief was harmful was explained by Alain Locke:

> Time out of mind he [the Negro actor] has been rated as a "natural-born actor" without any appreciation of what that statement, if true, really means. Often it was intended as a disparaging estimate of the Negro's limitations, a recognition of his restriction to interpretative as distinguished from the creative aspect of drama, a confinement, in terms of a second order of talent, to the status of the mimic and the clown.[28]

Locke cautioned, therefore, against the continued use of such misleading designations as "natural actors" precisely because they represented the type of subterfuge which had been instrumental in keeping his race mired in subordinate dramatic roles and forms.

Equally damaging to Negroes was the corollary belief, as expressed by no less a figure than W. E. B. DuBois, that this ethnic group was dramatic by nature.[29] Consequently, there should have been little surprise when such shallow thinking found its way into plays which examined the black man's expe-

[25]New York *Times,* July 24, 1938.

[26]The author of *Haiti* was a white New York City newspaperman, not the famed Negro Ph.D. from Harvard, W. E. B. DuBois.

[27]Isaacs, *The Negro in the American Theatre,* p. 79.

[28]Alain Locke, "American Theatre," in *Theatre: Essays on the Arts,* ed. Edith Isaacs (Boston: Little, Brown and Company, 1927), p. 120.

[29]W. E. B. DuBois, "The Drama Among Black Folk," *Crisis* 12 (August 1916): 169.

rience in this country. No playwright monopolized in presenting racial fantasies which contributed to the lowly status of Negroes in American society, but Nobel Prize winner Eugene O'Neill's distinction between the races in *All God's Chillun Got Wings* was certainly one of the most apocryphal.

> People pass, black and white, the Negroes frankly participants in the spirit of Spring, the whites laughing constrainedly, awkward in natural emotion. Their words are lost. One hears only their laughter. It expresses the difference in race.[30]

Depictions of this kind, whether authored by a white or a black playwright, were seldom questioned by theatregoers because they had been conditioned into accepting them. The frequency of such spurious portrayals, once the WPA theatre began operations, was drastically curtailed because the project's leadership made a concerted effort to guard against this development.[31] In the end, the Federal Theatre's interest in racial justice distinguished it from previous theatrical undertakings.

From the outset of the Federal Theatre, project officials initiated a very close working relationship with the nation's largest minority group. Consequently, the level of communication between these groups was consistently impressive throughout the project's duration. Whenever project administrators called for a meeting to formulate policy, they invariably made a point of inviting Negro representatives to such deliberations. In the event that these officials had been thinking in terms of bypassing blacks (and there is no evidence to indicate that this was considered), there still remained a Federal Theatre regulation which had made it mandatory "that there be racial representation in all national planning."[32] A black WPA administrator, Alfred E.

[30]Eugene O'Neill, "All God's Chillun Got Wings" (Federal Theatre Project script, 1924), act 1, scene 1, page 1.

[31]See Anne Powell, "The Negro and the Federal Theatre," *Crisis* 43 (November 1936): 340-342; and FTP Papers.

[32]This regulation was passed at a project workshop held at Vassar College in June 1937. Significantly, several Negroes, including Shirley Graham, Helen Tamiris, and Ruth Dunmore, were among the more than forty Federal Theatre Project personnel invited to attend the conference ("First Federal Summer Theatre: A Report," p. 33).

Smith, also kept a close surveillance on the developments within the theatre project because of his role as liaison between the Roosevelt administration and the Negro press. In the research department, Francis Bosworth and Rosamund Gilder actively sought the assistance of numerous individuals and organizations, including Walter White of the NAACP and Carter Woodson of the Association for the Study of Negro Life and History, in the critical matter of accumulating a reference file of acceptable Negro plays to be considered for production by the project's black units.[33] Then, too, Hallie Flanagan conferred with T. Arnold Hill in an attempt to find employment for approximately forty jobless young black playwrights who had only recently graduated from Negro colleges around the nation. The national director did not disappoint the untested dramatists; instead she immediately waived the WPA requisite for employment in the Federal Theatre (previous professional experience) because she recognized the importance of providing such potentially talented writers with an opportunity to learn their craft in an apprenticeship setting. That these efforts did not go unnoticed was demonstrated later, while the continued existence of the Federal Theatre was being debated in Congress, when over 150 Negro organizations signed an affidavit attesting to the equality of treatment meted out to blacks in the project.[34]

The Federal Theatre's attention to black concerns was not the only reason that Negro groups rallied behind this project when it was faced with possible extinction. That such support would be forthcoming in any emergency was assured earlier when blacks had the opportunity to determine their own course in the theatre project. At the time the project was first organized, for example, it was Rose McClendon who pointed the direction in which the black units would move; her suggestion that there be separate black units within the overall framework of the project became operative policy.[35] It was this same black spokeswoman who

[33] FTP Papers.

[34] Federal Theatre Project Brief Containing Detailed Answers to Charges Made by Witnesses Who Appeared Before the Special Committee to Investigate Un-American Activities (House of Representatives) FTP Papers.

[35] Allen F. Kifer, "The Negro Under the New Deal, 1933-1941" (Ph.D. dissertation, University of Wisconsin, 1964), p. 242.

argued against Miss Flanagan's attempt to extend the directorship of the Harlem unit to a Negro.[36]

The other black representatives in attendance at the conference—Edna Thomas, Harry Edwards, Carlton Moss, Abram Hill,
Jr., Augustus Smith, and Dick Campbell to mention the most
prominent—all concurred with their hostess's assessment that
the Harlem branch of the Federal Theatre should initially be
directed by a theatre-wise white.[37] It was understood by everyone at the meeting, however, that white leadership would give
way to black control once the minority group's requested apprenticeship period was completed. The responsibility for this
future transference of power was charged to the white leadership,
which was instructed to locate and train black replacements for
themselves. A similar pattern of securing directorial talent was
repeated in the project's remaining black units.[38]

Subsequent to the encouraging beginnings, there were several
additional indices which demonstrated the black participant's
seminal role in the project. The *Federal Theatre Magazine,*
hailed rather generously by Miss Flanagan as the best history of
the project, was halted by the WPA following publication of
eleven issues between November 1935 and July 1937. Government officials ascribed the stoppage to the fact that the three
other WPA art projects had no literary mouthpiece; but the
theatre project's national director read the censorship differently.[39]

Accorded wide—and highly favorable—exposure in the project's national publication, blacks also benefitted from the Federal
Theatre leadership's close surveillance of project activities.[40] In

[36]Hallie Flanagan, *Arena: The History of the Federal Theatre* (New York:
Duell, Sloan, and Pearce, 1940), p. 63.

[37]Two of these figures, Abram Hill and Dick Campbell, were instrumental
in the founding of the American Negro Theatre in 1940 following the demise of
the Federal Theatre.

[38]Consequently, there were several units which later had black directors,
including New York (J. Augustus Smith and Carlton Moss), Los Angeles (Clarence Muse), and Boston (Ralf Coleman). Another black, Theodore Browne, was
the assistant director of the Seattle Negro unit.

[39]Flanagan, *Arena,* pp. 204-205.

[40]Such monitoring was designed to assist units in their production tasks—
not stifle or censor individual initiative. It should be noted that nearly all the
cases involving censorship were those in which state WPA officials and not
theatre project administrators interfered with project activities.

this regard, inventorying project undertakings insured that the avowed objectives regarding Negro units were not overlooked. One inventory form pointedly requested whether the city's theatre project had a Negro unit, whereas another questionnaire surveyed the ethnic makeup of those playwrights already on the WPA payrolls.[41] Then, too, the Federal Theatre constantly consulted black spokesmen—in and out of the theatre—regarding project activities and the future direction of black theatre in this country. A letter from Rex Ingram to the national director, written in the waning days of the project, further indicated the extent to which the theatre project attempted to contribute to the development of black drama.[42]

Hence even as the Federal Theatre neared its termination date following Congressional action, the project's abiding concern for black theatre was indeed evident.

Perhaps the Federal Theatre's greatest contribution to the growth of Negro drama was its "honest attempt to develop black playwrights who could express life in their own vernacular."[43] Limited to writing part-time because of the necessity of earning a living as a dishwasher, custodian, housepainter, Pullman porter, redcap, or common laborer, the Negro writer's unseemly vocational fate was nicely underlined by Langston Hughes: "The steam in hotel kitchens/And the smoke in hotel lobbies/And the slime in hotel spittoons/Part of my life."[44] Government subsidy radically altered this employment pattern, however, by freeing black playwrights to learn and practice their craft on a full-time basis.

The Negro Dramatists' Laboratory, conceived by the managing directors of the Harlem project, was the most concentrated attempt by the WPA to encourage and develop black playwrights. Altogether some one-hundred promising black writers were invited to attend the New York-based symposium, but only fifty actually enrolled in the workshop. Lectures focused on such

[41] Federal Theatre Project, "Play Bureau Inventory" (New York: Works Progress Administration, 1939); and "First Federal Summer Theatre: A Report."

[42] Rex Ingram letter to Hallie Flanagan from Paris, France, June 20, 1939 (FTP Papers).

[43] Floyd Gaffney, "Black Theatre: Commitment and Communication," *The Black Scholar* 1 (June 1970): 10-11.

[44] Quoted by Roi Ottley in *The Negro in New York. An Informal Social History* (New York: New York Public Library, 1967), p. 255.

facets of the theatre as script forms, research techniques, technical requirements, and copyright laws. The critical importance of a play's thematic allegiance to the turbulent social conditions of the depression decade and the anticipated establishment of a permanent Negro theatre were also stressed at the 1936 conference, which was conducted by the New York project in conjunction with that city's professional and university theatre groups. The four-month long school spawned the remarkable total of eighteen full-length plays and five one-act dramas. All of these dramatic pieces were submitted to Negro units for production, and the Federal Theatre eventually produced two of them.[45]

But the New York undertaking was not the only laboratory experience provided aspiring black playwrights in the theatre project. Negro units elsewhere also supplied the type of apprenticeship necessary to develop skilled dramatists. Theodore Ward, the author of *Big White Fog* and one of the most successful black writers developed by the project, paid tribute to the Federal Theatre as a training ground for would-be playwrights, "to provide the literature which will serve as a basis for the full flowering of the Negro theatre."[46]

Ward, Hughes Allison, Theodore Browne, Ralf Coleman, Laura Edwards, Abram Hill, George Norford, Lew Payton, R. Washington Porter, John Silvera, J. Augustus Smith, and Frank Wilson all became resident dramatists with Negro units. Daily exposure to the total theatre environment certainly was invaluable to these budding craftsmen, as was the lengthy rehearsal period for Federal Theatre productions which allowed them to make necessary alterations in their scripts.[47] Black scholar Floyd Gaffney was not mistaken, therefore, when he recently wrote that the WPA project afforded Negro writers "an entree into American mainstream theatre for the first time."[48]

[45]Federal Theatre Project, "Report of the Activities and Accomplishments of Negro Dramatists Laboratory," (Washington, D.C., National Archives, Record Group 69).

[46]Brown, "The Federal Theatre," p. 103.

[47]The practice of lengthy rehearsals was criticized by Congressional committees investigating the Federal Theatre Project, even though developing untried playwrights was advertised as one of the major objectives of the project.

[48]Gaffney, "Black Theatre," p. 10.

Other than being accorded parity within the project itself, blacks also shared equal footing with white playgoers at Federal Theatre productions. According to Emmet Lavery, all WPA presentations were opened to the public without any racial restrictions. The director of the National Play Bureau further emphasized that project knowledge of the occurrence of any exclusionary practice would have resulted in an immediate correction.[49] And within the theatres themselves, Negroes were not relegated to the balconies either. Instead they were interspersed with whites on the basis of random seat procurement.[50] Moreover, government sponsorship drastically changed the pattern of attendance at black dramatic productions.[51]

Lastly, the project's social-minded perspective conditioned audiences into being more receptive to the problem play which explored contemporary conditions, a development previously discouraged by the Broadway-dominated commercial theatres because of box-office concerns.[52]

At last given a chance to assume center stage in the professional theatre in America, blacks compiled an outstanding record during their four years of participation on the WPA project. In fact, Negro unit productions so dominated Federal Theatre headlines that an overwhelming preponderance of contemporary observers adjudged their work as the best done on the project— this in a cultural field where qualitative assessments have rarely approached unanimity. Any listing of the project's premier plays has always included such black presentations as *Run, Little Chillun; Stevedore; Big White Fog; Macbeth;* and *The Swing Mikado*, with Hall Johnson's *Run, Little Chillun* staging commanding three-and-four dollar scalpers' prices for tickets to the Los Angeles production which had been priced at fifty-five cents—and this during the depression, too.[53] Behind this record

[49]Memorandum from Emmet Lavery, December 1, 1973.

[50]Robert Littell, "Everyone Likes Chocolate," *Vogue* 40 (November 1936): 66.

[51]Powell, "The Negro and the Federal Theatre," p. 341.

[52]Dick Campbell wrote Hallie Flanagan January 10, 1940 after the demise of the project that "audiences are most responsive and encouraging and seem to have awakened to a drama consciousness, which I can't help believe is the result of the Negro Federal Theatre productions in the past" (FTP Papers).

[53]Robert Holcomb, "The Federal Theatre in Los Angeles," *California Historical Society Quarterly* 41 (June 1962): 143.

of achievement by black participants stood their decidedly different perspective regarding government employment than that held by their more seasoned white counterparts. The black theatre critic, Fannin S. Belcher explained:

> It must be recognized, however, that there was a difference in attitude between the white and the Negro groups. The former, to a large extent, viewed the Federal Theatre Project merely as a temporary job to tide them over the lull in stage activities; the latter were securing their first opportunity to have steady employment in their profession, to produce the plays they wanted to produce without bowing to commercial prejudices and were hoping to do so well that the group might be self-supporting if and when Federal Theatre was dissolved. The Negro units also thought of the project as a training school.[54]

Having previously been assigned an inferior position in the American theatre, blacks subsequently took full advantage of their first extended opportunity in the professional theatre. In the process, they demonstrated conclusively that playwriting, directing, stage designing, and serious acting were well within their province—all they had ever needed was the chance that the Federal Theatre Project provided them.

[54]Fannin S. Belcher, "The Place of the Negro in the Evolution of the American Theatre, 1767-1940" (Ph.D. dissertation, Yale University, 1945), pp. 419-420.

# The American Negro Theatre

## by *Ethel Pitts Walker*

The establishment of the American Negro Theatre (A.N.T.) was the fulfillment of a dream by Black theatre artists in search of a home to practice their art. Unable to find a place on the Broadway stage, these artists turned to the Harlem community. They created in Harlem an active, dynamic theatre, one that introduced new playwrights, trained actors and technicians, produced a number of significant dramas, and built Black audiences for the live theatre. These achievements have gained the A.N.T. an honored place in the history of Black theatre in America.

The story of the A.N.T. begins in 1940 with Abram Hill and Frederick O'Neal. Both men came from theatrical backgrounds and had worked in community and professional theatre. They disapproved of the ingrained star-system in the professional theatre with its limited opportunities for Blacks. When the Federal Theatre Project of the Works Progress Administration ended in 1939, Black theatre artists who had been employed in Negro units across the country were thrown back on their own resources. Hill and O'Neal felt that what was needed was a community-based theatre, a theatre not dominated by the actor but one where directors, writers, technicians and actors were equally important and where there would be a training program for young theatre artists. They set out to establish such an institution in Harlem.[1]

"The American Negro Theatre" by Ethel Pitts Walker. This article appears for the first time in this volume. Reprinted by permission of the author.

[1]Abram Hill, interviewed by Mischell Wallace, January 19, 1974, at his home in New York City. Tape available in Hatch-Billops Studios, Inc., New York, N.Y. Reviewed by Ethel Pitts Walker.

Abram Hill was born in Atlanta, Georgia, in 1914 and moved with his family to New York in the 1920s. As a teenager he worked as a photographer's assistant and in his spare time wrote short stories and a novel.[2] For a time he served as a drama coach to church groups in Harlem before entering Lincoln University in Pennsylvania in 1934. While at Lincoln he took courses in English and drama, using his spare time to write, stage and direct plays. Since Lincoln offered no drama major, Hill graduated with a B.A. in English.

Hill developed his playwriting skills during the time he worked as drama director with a unit of the Temporary Emergency Relief Association in Long Island. In an effort to produce shows for the camp, he began to adapt available plays to the Black experience, revising and rewriting a number of scripts. The need for plays about Black life eventually led him to write original scripts based on the experiences of the young people with whom he worked. In 1938 he received a scholarship to the New School for Social Research where he studied drama under Teresa Hillsbury and John Gassner. He had earlier submitted a one-act play, *Hell's Half Acre,* in the Theatre Guild contest. Although he did not win a prize, Hillsbury and Gassner had written that they believed he had considerable potential as a playwright. Among the young playwrights studying with Gassner at the time were Tennessee Williams and Arthur Miller.[3]

When the Federal Theatre Project started, Hill accepted a position in the playreading and playwriting department. He read scripts that dealt mainly with Black themes and characters and prepared critical analyses of them for potential directors and producers. He was also assigned to write a history of Black life for the Living Newspaper Unit. However the controversy involving communists within the Federal Theatre prevented his script, *Liberty Deferred,* from reaching the stage before the Federal Theatre was itself dismantled.[4]

Hill began to seek work in the professional theatre and, unable to find a position on Broadway, he turned to Harlem. At this time the Rose McClendon Players under the direction of

[2]Anna Rothe, ed., *Current Biography 1945* (New York: The H. W. Wilson Co., 1946), p. 283.
[3]Abram Hill, interviewed by Mischell Wallace.
[4]*Ibid.*

Dick Campbell dominated the Harlem theatre scene. Hill showed his new play, *On Striver's Row*, to Campbell and, after some cutting and polishing, the McClendon Players produced it in 1939.[5] In his search for a theatre not geared primarily to the actor, Hill shared his ideas with several Black playwrights including Hugh Allison, Theodore Ward, Powell Lindsay, Langston Hughes and George Norford. They discussed the state of Black theatre in America and decided they would form a group called the Negro Playwrights Company. In the summer of 1940 this new group announced their first production; it was to be Theodore Ward's play *Big White Fog*. However, by this time Abram Hill had left the organization because, in his view, the founding members seemed too willing to sacrifice artistic quality for propaganda.[6] Hill began looking once more for a theatrical home.

Among the cast of the McClendon Players' production of *On Striver's Row* was Frederick O'Neal. Born in Brooksville, Mississippi, in 1905, O'Neal had attended public school in St. Louis, Missouri, created neighborhood shows at the age of nine, and by thirteen, had already decided on a career in the theatre.[7] His first professional appearance was as Silvius in Shakespeare's *As You Like It,* the play selected for the annual production of the St. Louis Urban League. Of his performance the *St. Louis Argus* of November 12, 1927, reported that O'Neal "handled his part well and aided in giving the play a well-rounded presentation." During this period he organized the Ira Aldridge Players and attempted to initiate a training program for the young actors, believing that "you never stop learning in theatre; in any group ...you have to have some kind of classes or school connected with it."[8] The training program petered out when the actor-students failed to show up for classes and the instructors resigned.[9] Nevertheless, the idea of a teaching program in the theatre arts became an important part of O'Neal's hope for a Negro theatre.

---

[5]*Ibid.*

[6]*Ibid.*

[7]Frederick O'Neal, interviewed by James Hatch, February 8, 1972, in New York City. Tape available in Hatch-Billops Studios, Inc., New York, N.Y. Reviewed by Ethel Pitts Walker.

[8]*Ibid.*

[9]Loften Mitchell, *Voices of the Black Theatre* (New Jersey: James T. White & Co., 1975), p. 175.

Encouraged by Zora Neale Hurston to come to New York, O'Neal was by 1936 appearing in the Civic Repertory Company's production of *Twenty Million Others*. At the same time, true to his belief in continuing theatre education, he enrolled at the New Theatre School and the American Theatre Wing. He also studied privately with Theodore Komisarjevsky.[10] In 1940 O'Neal and Abram Hill began to talk seriously about organizing a new theatre in Harlem. They agreed on an approach that would result in a cooperative organization not dominated by any one person. The theatre would have a training program and would emphasize all phases of theatrical activity, not just acting. They interested a number of people in the idea and sent out postcards inviting several more to attend their first meeting.

On June 11, 1940, the group met and eighteen people present formed the American Negro Theatre.[11] Membership increased steadily to about thirty. Some of the original members of the company were Howard Augusta, Ruby Dee, Samuel Greene, Betty Haynes, James Jackson, George Lewis, Claire Leyba, Kenneth Mannigault, Helen Martin and Virgil Richardson.[12] The organization made several important decisions; chief among them was the determination to avoid being influenced by the star system. As Abram Hill explained later:

> Frederick O'Neal, co-founder of A.N.T., often said at weekly meetings: "A.N.T. is not a star-making organization. One may play a leading role in one production and be an attendant in the rest room during the following presentation. ... Stardom is a by-product of the highest individual achievement and can be bestowed upon you by ranks beyond this organization. *We* are a theatrical family. The family, not the individual, is the star."[13]

It was this conviction that led the group to choose the name

[10]Freda Gaye, ed., *Who's Who in the Theatre, 14th ed.* (London: Pitman Publishing Co., 1970), p. 1033.

[11]Abram Hill, interviewed by Mischell Wallace. O'Neal states in his interview with Hatch that they originally sent out thirty postcards and that twenty-eight of the thirty people showed up for the first meeting.

[12] Claire Leyba, interviewed by Ethel Pitts Walker, January 4, 1975, at her home in New York City.

[13]Loften Mitchell, *Voices*, p. 123.

American Negro Theatre. The acronym A.N.T. meant that all members had pledged to be like ants, real workers.[14]

Abram Hill became director of the company and remained in office until he resigned in 1948. He also served as chairman of the Executive Committee. Fred O'Neal was assistant chairman and company manager. Other officers were J. Deveaux Davis as business manager, Oliver Harrington as art director, Martha Sherrill as voice and speech director and Vivian Hall as secretary.[15] The need to provide a facility for Black theatre artists in Harlem dominated the thinking and planning of the company. They secured permission to perform in the little theatre of the 135th Street Library—a converted lecture room seating about 125—that had housed several earlier Negro theatre groups such as the Krigwa Players, the Harlem Suitcase Theatre and the Rose McClendon Players.

The founders of A.N.T. hoped "to break down the barriers of Black participation in the theatre; to portray Negro life as they honestly saw it; to fill in the gap of a Black theatre which did not exist."[16] Although the theatre was formed initially to reflect the Harlem community, it was never a segregated organization. A.N.T. member Claire Leyba explained that the company never became concerned about Black and White since they hired White teachers and accepted White actors and technicians.[17] Nevertheless, the idea of a theatre in Harlem for Black people was central to the conception of A.N.T. As Alice Childress has said: "We thought we were Harlem's theatre."[18]

The need to establish a strong organization was felt early. Discipline became important and members paid fines for being late to rehearsal. Members who performed outside A.N.T. were required to pay two percent of their salary into the company's account in order to keep it solvent. Everyone realized that survival depended on a close, family relationship and all worked

---

[14] Abram Hill, interviewed by Mischell Wallace.

[15] From *Hits, Bits, and Skits* program in Claire Leyba's scrapbook.

[16] Abram Hill, interviewed by Mischell Wallace.

[17] Claire Leyba, interviewed by Ethel Pitts Walker.

[18] Alice Childress, interviewed by James Hatch, February 21, 1972, at her home in New York City. Tape available in the Hatch-Billops Studios, Inc., New York, N.Y. Reviewed by Ethel Pitts Walker.

together to make the venture a success. Claire Leyba related the
enthusiasm and love the members shared for A.N.T.: "I used to
get things from my mother's trunk and Helen Martin used to
bring things from home."[19] The company was an incorporated
cooperative with all members sharing expenses or profits. Except for a period of three years when part-time salaries were paid
to some officers under a foundation grant, no one received com-
pensation for their work in the company. Despite the lack of
funding, the company raised enough money to finance its productions, trained over 200 people and attracted some fifty
thousand patrons to witness 325 performances.[20]

In 1944 A.N.T. applied to the General Education Board of the
Rockefeller Foundation for financial support. The grant proposal
recommended that salaries be paid to some of the company's
officers, most of whose time was devoted to the affairs of the
group. In addition, the proposal set forth the following objectives by which A.N.T. activities should be measured:

1. *To Develop an Art.* A permanent acting company [coor-
dinating] and perfecting the related arts of the theatre; eventually
deriving its own theatre craft and acting style by combining all
standard forms and putting to artful use the fluency and rhythm
that lie in the Negro's special gifts.[21]

2. *To Develop a Vital Theatre.* Calling for plays which furnish
commentary, interpretation, illumination and criticism of our
common lives during contemporary times, located in the Harlem
section of New York City, with its theatre, workshop and school
affiliated with Negro theatre groups throughout the country, and
acting as a parent body to such affiliates.

3. *To Develop Pride and Honor.* For a theatre which for too long
has been unstudied and exploited; by being honest, yet unflat-
tering, by being perfectionists rather than professionals, and win-
ning the pride of the people rather than their apathy.[22]

[19]Claire Leyba, interviewed by Ethel Pitts Walker.
[20]Loften Mitchell, *Voices,* p. 118.
[21]In Mischell Wallace's interview with Abram Hill, Hill explained that A.N.T.
recognized the Negro had certain potential as an entertainer in the theatre, and
the essence of that in those days was a certain rhythmic quality and a certain
animation that most ethnic groups didn't have at that time.
[22]Abram Hill, proposal submitted to the General Education Board of the
Rockefeller Foundation, New York, N.Y., February 25, 1944.

These objectives were printed on A.N.T. production programs. The company had made its case convincingly to the Foundation and received a grant-in-aid of $22,000.[23] A.N.T. divided its program into three areas: (i) stage productions; (ii) training workshops and a school of drama; and (iii) radio shows. O'Neal felt that each activity proved to be a unique experience for the participants.[24] The company held two variety shows to raise funds and introduce the new theatre to the Harlem community. The first show, *Hits, Bits, and Skits,* opened on July 17, 1940, and the second on February 7, 1941. From 1940 to 1949 the company produced nineteen plays, twelve of which were original scripts.[25] According to Hill, four of their productions transferred from A.N.T. to the commercial theatre. These were *On Striver's Row, Anna Lucasta, Walk Hard,* and *Freight.*[26] The willingness of the company to experiment in the production of original scripts established it as a unique theatre in New York. This feature received general endorsement from theatre critics:

> It is...a healthy experimental theatre, one that at all costs strives to avoid conventional Broadway-born cliches. ... It remains firmly on the ground, using themes about everyday people, staged and played with originality and imagination.[27]

During the latter years of the company's existence, this basic concept of experimentation faded and A.N.T. turned to more traditional works.

Of the nineteen legitimate dramas produced, Black writers included Abram Hill, Theodore Browne, and Owen Dodson. After 1945, all plays produced were by White writers, many of whom dealt with Black life. In addition to the three mentioned above, the major playwrights whose work was produced by A.N.T. in-

---

[23]Loften Mitchell, *Voices,* p. 126.

[24]Frederick O'Neal, interviewed by Ethel Pitts Walker.

[25]Original scripts included Curtis Cooksey's *Starlight,* Philip Yordan's *Anna Lucasta,* Abram Hill's *Walk Hard,* Owen Dodson's *Garden of Time,* Dan Hammerman's *Henri Christophe,* Samuel M. Kootz's *Home Is the Hunter,* Kurt Unkelbach's *The Peacemakers,* Katherine Garrison's *Sojourner Truth,* Walter Carroll's *Tin Top Valley,* Nat Sherman's *The Washington Years,* Jonathan Tree's *The Fisherman,* and Kenneth White's *Freight.*

[26]Abram Hill, interviewed by Ethel Pitts Walker, January 6, 1975, in New York City.

[27]Jack Hamilton, "The American Negro Theatre," *Dramatics,* March, 1946, p. 3.

cluded Philip Yordan and Kenneth White. As artistic director of the company, Abram Hill directed five productions, two of them, *On Striver's Row* and *Walk Hard,* being his own plays. The first play is a satire on social climbing and the second dealt with the racial problems encountered by a young Black who wishes to be a prizefighter. The other three plays directed by Hill were *Three's a Family, Home Is the Hunter,* and *Tin Top Valley.* Apart from these and Osceola Archer's production of *Sojourner Truth,* other major productions were directed by guest directors from the commercial and university theatres whom A.N.T. invited to work with the company. Occasionally a playwright would direct his own script.

A.N.T. produced its most significant and successful plays during its first five years of existence from 1940 to 1945. The first major production, Hill's *On Striver's Row,* became the company's most popular attraction and was twice revived.[28] The premier production ran for five months in weekend performances and by December 1940 approximately five thousand people had seen the show. Excerpts from it were broadcast over WLTH on Sundays.[29] A.N.T.'s second production, Browne's *Natural Man,* was also well received by Harlem audiences. The play is based on the John Henry legends of the Deep South and included music and dancing. Fred O'Neal called it the company's "most significant play."[30] George Freedley of the *Morning Telegraph* praised the acting performances of Ruby Wallace and Stanley Greene. He wrote that "the whole production was filled with inventive acting which was worthy of any Broadway playhouse."[31]

History of a sort was made in November 1943 when A.N.T. produced Phoebe and Henry Ephron's play *Three's a Family* at the 135th Street Library Theatre. At the same time, a White cast was appearing in the play at the Longacre Theatre on Broadway. The producer, John Golden, invited the Harlem group to bring their production downtown for a one night benefit performance. On April 17, 1944, A.N.T. performed the play at the Longacre Theatre, becoming the first Black company to stage a play on

---

[28]*On Striver's Row* was revived as a musical in 1941.
[29]*New York Amsterdam News,* December 21, 1940, p. 21.
[30]Frederick O'Neal, interviewed by Ethel Pitts Walker.
[31]George Freedley, "The Stage Today," *Morning Telegraph,* May 9, 1941, p. 15.

Broadway simultaneously with a White company.[32] Reporter Julius Adams wrote: "the capacity crowd that witnessed the play gave every evidence of having been thrilled by the performance which was in every sense of the word up to Broadway standards.[33] But the play that marked a turning point in the fortunes of the American Negro Theatre was Philip Yordan's *Anna Lucasta,* first produced at the Library Theatre in Harlem in 1944. The play was originally written about a Polish-American family and was extensively revised by Abram Hill and the director, Harry Gribble, for a Black cast. It was a great hit. Within weeks with some recasting and further rewriting the production was moved to Broadway where it opened at the Mansfield Theatre on August 30. With Hilda Simms in the title role, Fred O'Neal and the imported Canada Lee in the cast, the play was a tremendous success.

Among the voices of acclaim from the critics, one writer struck a cautionary note that proved to be prophetic. Writing in the *Brooklyn Daily Eagle* of September 18, 1944, Arthur Pollock raised several pertinent questions:

> In the first place, the play isn't exactly what it was when they did it by themselves. Is that good or is it bad? Does it represent their ideals? Have they gone Broadway? Honest groups like this worry about such things. For such things can ruin them. They may find that they are thinking of the theater in terms solely commercial. ... It has succeeded with the play at the Mansfield. But that play's author is not a Negro. Shall it go on producing plays of whites as well as Negroes? Shall it be content so long as the plays have something to say about Negroes?

Speaking some three decades later, Abram Hill summarized in words a response to those questions which had long since been answered by the bitter experiences of A.N.T. following its biggest success:

> *Anna* was a history-making event. It put the organization on the map and ironically it planted the seeds of destruction. For, from that point on the organization was going downhill. People came into it after that trying to get to Broadway. The A.N.T. became a showcase instead of an experimental theatre. ... From two films and

[32]*New York Amsterdam News,* April 15, 1944, p. 1.

[33]Julius J. Adams, "Broadway Trek by A.N.T. Heralded as Great Achievement by Negro, *New York Amsterdam News,* April 22, 1944, p. 1-A.

many English-speaking productions—and I think even a Yiddish version was done in Israel later—I can't imagine what this venture has really earned. Within two years the play had grossed seven million through the national company and the local company.... We were getting 1 ¼ percent on only the Broadway production.[34]

The financial arrangements caused controversy and dissension among A.N.T. members and John Wildberg, the Broadway producer of the play. Original cast members in the Harlem production who were not chosen for downtown were "never happy again." Others like Miss Simms and Fred O'Neal gained unequalled success as actors. The play brought Broadway critics to the Harlem theatre in record number and future productions were judged in terms of Broadway fare. After 1945 the company produced a series of mediocre plays and received a series of mediocre reviews. Nothing was quite the same for A.N.T.

From the beginning A.N.T. established workshops in theatre skills for its members, and ninety percent of the active membership received its basic training in the company.[35] Those actors who had begun work with other small theatre groups developed their talents with A.N.T. Instructors included Nadya Ramanov, Doris Sorrell and Alvin Childress. Former A.N.T. actors who became prominent in their profession are Alice Childress, Ruby Dee, Gordon Heath, Earle Hyman, Fred O'Neal, Hilda Simms, Muriel Smith and Clarice Taylor, among others.

Few Black trained technicians existed in the theatres of the 1940s. Only one Black, Perry Watkins, belonged to the designer's union. A.N.T. wanted to develop technicians as well as actors and encouraged potential designers, such as Roger Furman, to confer regularly with Broadway designers.[36] Besides Furman, other designers for the company included Charles Sebree, S. Sanford Engel, A. A. Ostrander, Richard Brown and Ralph Alswang. Perry Watkins served as technical director for Hill's *Walk Hard*.

Within two years of its inception, A.N.T. started a school of drama. Located in the Waldleigh High School at 215 West 11th Street, the A.N.T. Studio Theatre became the first Black theatre institution to be incorporated by the New York State Board of

[34] Loften Mitchell, *Voices*, p. 131.
[35] Abram Hill, Report of A.N.T. Inc., to the General Education Board of the Rockefeller Foundation, New York, N.Y., December, 1947.
[36] Abram Hill, interviewed by Ethel Pitts Walker.

Education.[37] Abram Hill asked Osceola Archer to head the school. Offering courses in acting, body movement, voice and speech, stagecraft, choral singing, playwriting and radio, the school sought to develop "completely-rounded" actors, knowledgeable and trained in every aspect of the theatre. The Studio Theatre had its own production program and its students presented such dramas as Wilder's *Our Town,* Gabrielson's *Days of Our Youth,* and Ferber and Kaufman's *Stage Door.* Sidney Poitier and Harry Belafonte are both alumni of the A.N.T. Studio program.

In 1945 the American Negro Theatre launched a new venture: it became the first Black theatrical company to present a regular radio series.[38] Under the guidance of Ted Cott, program director, and Jack Grogan, production director, A.N.T. began a Sunday afternoon radio program called "New World A-Coming." The station, WNEW, established a policy designed to promote the universality of scripts, characters and performing talent:

> At no time during the performance of the air dramas and comedies will an effort be made to over-exploit the series as a Negro venture. The important thing at all times will be the play and not the fact that it is being presented by a group of Negro performers...A.N.T. will be mentioned only at the end of each show.[39]

The company received excellent reviews as they presented both dramas and operas. The thirty-minute series utilized the talents of A.N.T. members as well as guest artists such as Canada Lee. The primary significance of the radio shows lay in the company's pioneering effort to present plays over the air without reference to race.

By 1950 the American Negro Theatre found itself with a well-earned reputation and a company of nonperforming artists. The company produced no plays that year and announced that it was in the process of reorganizing. It was never to rebound from the artistic slump that had set in.

Of all the factors contributing to A.N.T.'s decline, the most

---

[37] Osceola Archer, interviewed by Ethel Pitts Walker, February 27, 1975, at her home in New York City.

[38] *Variety,* September 26, 1945, p. 36.

[39] *New York Age,* September 22, 1945, p. 11. Jack Gould of *The New York Times,* October 7, 1945, Sec. 2, p. 5, disagrees with announcing of A.N.T. at the end of each program. Other companies receive recognition at the beginning and Gould feels WNEW should not make an exception for A.N.T.

commonly acknowledged is the success of *Anna Lucasta*. Fred O'Neal opined that "*Anna* was the company's greatest failure. ... It took the main company to Broadway and they never came back."[40] Success also brought hordes of new members all searching for their chance to reach Broadway but with little of the commitment or community spirit that had brought the group together in the first place. "Everyone," Hill said later, "had caught the professional bug."[41] Another important factor in A.N.T.'s decline centered around the eventual conflict of aims. Hill explained that a conflict arose between actors and playwrights: the actors looked toward a professional career in commercial theatre and the playwrights looked to the community. A.N.T. members would leave a show in rehearsal to accept a Broadway role.[42] The idea of a theatre geared to meet the needs of the Harlem community took a back seat to a theatre geared to send actors to the Great White Way.

Not only did *Anna Lucasta* draw many new applicants to A.N.T., it also placed the company in competition with the professional theatre downtown. Critics began to judge A.N.T. productions by commercial standards and "people came to Harlem no longer to witness vital theatre but to look for something that would 'sell downtown.'"[43] As A.N.T.'s reputation grew, the major theatre critics from such newspapers as *Variety* and the *New York Times* consistently covered its productions and compared them to *Anna Lucasta*. Attention turned from the Harlem community to Broadway.

A.N.T. also suffered financial difficulties, especially during its latter years. The Rockefeller Foundation grant had expired by December 31, 1947, and the group had to rely on its box office receipts and on contributions.[44] Some months after the *Anna Lucasta* production, the company was asked to move from the Library Theatre which it had inhabited for five years without

[40] Frederick O'Neal, interviewed by Ethel Pitts Walker.
[41] Abram Hill, interviewed by Mischell Wallace.
[42] *Ibid.*
[43] Loften Mitchell, *Black Drama* (New York: Hawthorn Books, Inc., 1967), p. 135.
[44] Abram Hill quoted in "Abe Hill Resigns As Director of A.N.T." by Dan Burley in *New York Amsterdam News*, February 28, 1948, p. 23.

cost. In new quarters it had to meet high rental charges, high utility bills, and high production expenses. The group even invested $5,000 in stocks in an attempt to improve its solvency and received only $600 or $700 back.[45] A.N.T. found itself with serious financial problems and no significant outside help. The company had begun its theatrical history with a series of variety shows. Now, ironically, in the fifties it turned to skits and variety shows again. Its theatre was moved from the 135th Street Library to Elks Lodge on West 126th Street, then to its final destination: a loft on West 125th Street. Paying fifty dollars a week and charging fifty cents a drink, the company never again produced any significant theatre.[46] The dream of its founders had ended without ceremony.

The American Negro Theatre created excitement in Harlem with the promise of a firmly established community theatre. That excitement could have existed for several more years, but it was short-lived. As long as A.N.T. performed its two or three productions a year in the 135th Street Library Theatre, as long as the company remained small in size and concentrated on Harlem rather than Broadway, the quality of its productions and the support of the community were of a high order. Once the company lost sight of its initial objectives, set its sights on Broadway, and expanded its programs to a full-time school and a weekly radio series, the group began to decrease in excellence. The initial energy for creating a theatre for Black people waned as the company gained in popularity and the actors reached for stardom. As its original focus changed, the company lost its creativity and impact. Nevertheless, A.N.T. provided a historic page in the development of the Black theatre movement:

> There was a great social revolution underway, the plays of protest, the plays of social meaning, and this was the kind of theatre we were trying to develop. Not just for entertainment and our own professional growth and artistry, but we wanted to say something significant and meaningful to the people.... We were a people's theatre. We would have certain family nights—five members of a

---

[45] Maxwell Glanville, interviewed by Ethel Pitts Walker, February 27, 1975, at his home in New York City.
[46] *Ibid.*

family would come in for one dollar. We'd cater to the churches, the schools and groups that would buy out the whole house. ... We were trying to say something. We were trying to say it within the black media, with the rhythm and the quality of excitement.[47]

[47] Loften Mitchell, *Voices,* p. 147.

# Black Theater in the South:
# Report and Reflections

*by Tom Dent*

The current state of Black theater in the South is the same as the current state of Black theater in America: ailing. In serious condition. The situation, after promising beginnings, is touch and go.

The object of our concern had its real beginnings in the sixties, and for our purposes we should look at two main thrusts. The first was characterized by a wealth of new plays about Afro-American life which hit the New York stage in the middle and late sixties. We could cite Lorraine Hansberry's *Raisin in the Sun* or Ossie Davis' *Purlie Victorious* as progenitors. We should also cite the creation of two major New York black repertory companies—the New Lafayette Theater (now closed) and the Negro Ensemble Company as landmarks of that New York thrust. We could say that Black theater in New York has been directed at the *general* theater-going public and theatrical establishment, though it doubtless has expanded the Black theater audience and economic opportunities for Black artists.

The second thrust has to do with Black community ensembles, also a child of the sixties, in cities and communities all over Afro-America. It is here that we want to focus our attention, and it is these groups that are, in my opinion, in trouble. Not that Black theater in New York doesn't have its problems; but theater in New York is primarily a commercial scene, and as long as there is commerce—something people will pay to see—there will be activity. The situation with community ensembles is essentially

"Black Theater in the South: Report and Reflections" by Tom Dent. From *Freedomways*, Vol. 14, No. 3 (1974), pp. 247-54. Reprinted by permission of *Freedomways* magazine, published at 799 Broadway, New York City.

different. Most do not have incomes or budgets to pay performers, nor is it possible for them to subsist from the box office; and, most importantly, their audience is almost entirely Black, which, as we will discuss, is of extreme significance.

It is to this second group, *Black community ensembles,* that southern theaters belong, and they have contributed a short but notable history.

It is ten years now since the Free Southern Theater was organized in Jackson, Mississippi, in the height of the southern freedom movement. Its objectives were concisely stated.

> ...to stimulate creative and reflective thought among Negroes in Mississippi and other southern states by the establishment of a legitimate theater, thereby providing the opportunity for involvement in the theater and the associated art forms.
>
> We theorize that within the Southern situation a theatrical form and style can be developed that is unique to the Negro people as the origin of blues and jazz.
>
> A combination of art and social awareness can evolve into plays written for a Negro audience, which relate to the problems within the Negro himself, and within the Negro community.

Usually a Prospectus is just so much meaningless rhetoric, but this statement by SNCC workers Doris Derby, Gilbert Moses and John O'Neal contained within it the germ of the potential of Black community theaters: (1) a new Black cultural consciousness among the people; (2) the potential to make a *new theater,* African-influenced in form as well as theme; (3) the presence of the Black audience as the compelling factor toward number two; (4) the prophetic suggestion that Black theater should take Black music as its ideal model for development; (5) the idea that a major concern of mature Black theater, as with Black music, must be contained in the Black-to-Black communication, "...the problems *within* the Negro himself,...within the Negro community."

That these objectives were not realized is not news; indeed realization in so short a time would be a lot to expect. As Larry Neal remarks in his perceptive review, *The Free Southern Theater by the Free Southern Theater,* it "had to spend several years hacking away at the deadwood of American liberal and aesthetic ideas." (*The Drama Review,* 1970, p. 172)

Despite the problems, the FST has a substantial and important history. Originally an integrated troupe, reflecting that phase of the civil rights movement, the FST in 1964, 1965 and 1966 was the first theater Black people in Mississippi had seen. Unfortunately, the first production, Duberman's *In White America,* set in motion the conflict over choice of material which has raged within the organization since it first had to deal with practicalities. *In White America* dealt with the *theme* of the Black saga in America, but was hardly a Black play in *form,* though the performance was livened by individual and ensemble songs.

In 1965, the FST settled in New Orleans. Though it continued to tour Mississippi in the summers, it turned increasingly to the problem of providing workshops and performances for New Orleans' large and talented Black community. From 1965 until now the FST has passed through many phases. Though change has been its constant, it has strongly reflected the dynamics of the national Black movement, becoming itself a Black community theater in New Orleans by 1967. The settling of the FST in New Orleans was itself a problem for many of the old members and supporters. New ensemble members saw the theater from the perspective of living in and knowing the needs of the Black South. The conflicts over direction and choice of material were intensified rather than eased. In my opinion, they never were satisfactorily resolved.

The Free Southern spawned a widening consciousness of theater as a potential form for the Black arts in the South. It also gave birth to the careers of several artists who achieved notable success in commercial theater and cinema.

The FST was only partially responsible for the growth of other community ensembles which sprang up in the South in the late sixties and early seventies. These new groups—Theater of Afro-Arts and "M" Ensemble in Miami; Sudan and Urban Theater in Houston; Black Image in Atlanta; Dashiki in New Orleans; and teenage poetry ensembles in Greenville, Miss., are the most notable—would have come into existence anyhow. They should be seen as part of the national community ensemble movement cited earlier.

The new southern groups, like their national counterparts, primarily perform scripts which were premiered at NEC [Negro Ensemble Company], New Lafayette, or at Off-Broadway theaters. From time to time, they have written their own material.

Sudan, which is not as active as it once was, is comprised solely of poets and performs its own material exclusively. TAA is notable for the stability of its voluntary ensemble, soundly led by Wendell Narcisse. Dashiki, now six years old, has achieved an extremely cohesive team of experienced community actors under the leadership of former Dillard University drama director Ted Gilliam. They perform with a regularity and quality probably unequalled by any other Black community ensemble in the nation. The FST, under the continual directorship of John O'Neal, has branched out into television and radio, and has concentrated, in the last two years, primarily on O'Neal's own scripts. Black Image seems to have phased out. "M" Ensemble has recently split into two groups; and their future at this time is unpredictable. All groups —except the FST which continues to receive some Foundation support—have budgets of $10,000 per year or less and are comprised of volunteer workers.

### Greater Impact Necessary

So much for the current situation. But what of the deeper question? How effective are these groups? Have they achieved a foothold in the Black community as institutions Black people need and turn to for aesthetic and meditative answers, as the people turn to "blues and jazz," the church, dance, TV, or cinema —sloppy and destructive as we may view these media?

My opinion is that none of the southern groups has as yet had impact on the man on the street. Neither, in fact, have the Black community theaters anywhere. As for the New York theaters, they play to an integrated audience where the Blacks are often a specialized and intellectual group. The record of New Lafayette in relating to the people of Harlem does not seem to be good, which may be one strong reason why New Lafayette does not exist today.

Plays with Black themes have proven they can survive in New York because New York is large and has a substantial theatergoing public. But the Black community ensembles, especially those in the South who play to an almost exclusively Black audience, cannot, in my opinion, survive unless they relate better to their audience.

I know that many will not agree with, or feel comfortable with, this opinion. It is true that the Black community ensemble movement is young, the theaters are underfunded, and despite the fact that theater is not a *popular* art form anywhere in America, Black ensembles have, through unusual commitment, built small followings. But I think the basic problem lies elsewhere. It has to do with the fact that the play form, the so-called "well made play," is not endemic to Black culture. The traditional play form is the product of western European art and culture. Herein lies the old contradiction within FST; and the same contradiction plagues all Black theaters when they must communicate with Black audiences.

Some of us (I worked with the FST for five years) were continually dissatisfied with the plays that seemed to be available for the FST to perform. In an effort to deal with this we began, in 1968, to try to develop new material for the theater. The mechanism for this was a workshop which we called BLKARTSOUTH. It was a writers' *and* actors' workshop by fortuitous accident, since there were so few people attending both originally separate workshops that we combined them into a single, longer session.

We hoped for relevant scripts in the traditional play form, but we found that most of the new work was poetry. So what to do with this poetry? We decided to put together an inexpensive magazine, which we called *Echoes From the Gumbo,* later *NKOMBO.* But then we hit on the idea of reading the poetry for audiences as a type of performance, something that seemed to develop naturally from writers reading their own work in the workshop and an increased emphasis on delivery, which stemmed from our practice of workshop members reading through new scripts. Thus, the writer could see immediately what his play looked and sounded like on stage. In other words, after only a few months, we began to think of everything we wrote in oral and performance terms, rather than purely literary and personal terms. We began to do poetry performances at Black arts festivals, commemorative programs, community meetings—the types of occasions the theater usually performed for. Instead of reading spontaneously, we found it necessary to organize and structure the poems, trying to mix types, humorous and serious, long and short, personal and generic, so that the poems reflected off each other, relating thematically to what preceded and followed. All of the work dealt with Black consciousness, Black reality, Black definition. We were excited by the response of audiences, particularly young audiences. When things were going well we experienced an immediacy of audience response (we used to call it *the vibes*), warm and instantaneous. It was as if the audience, even though they had never previously experienced something we could call a "poetry reading," understood what was happening, could relate to it, could respond to it with an enthusiasm that surprised and encouraged us.

So we went on, further developing and refining. We broke down the material into thematic sections, usually three. The first might deal with racial loss of identity and impotence, the second with the beauties and rewards of the Black life style, Black love of self and family, and the conclusion, with Black positiveness, assertion, and power. As our performances became more frequent, we added ensemble poems embroidered with chants and interchanged lines, audience response poems and music, both vocal and guitar, and narration over instrumental music and humming. And we began to do something else, almost unconsciously. Since we had more poems than we could possibly use for a single performance, we learned to check out the audience before the performance and pull out or add material based on how we sized up the audience and how we wanted to affect them. By 1970, we knew pretty well how to *play* an audience, inserting material that would be relevant and removing material we thought irrelevant.

The next stage of development happened naturally. We began to think of the poems as more than an oral device; it seemed that the meaning would be clearer if one or more of the members not reading (never more than five altogether) assumed harmony, dialogue and mimetic roles in relationship to the poem or the reader—similar to the routines of Black soul music groups in support of the lead singer. If the poem asked a question, one of the poets might say "What?" or "Why?," setting up the conclusion of the poem, keeping it free from seeming over-rehearsed, in fact, attempting to preserve the illusion of spontaneity even though the audience knew we were working from prepared material. This is the Black style: emotion, broad humor, and individual improvisation against group harmony. Soon after we reached this point, for reasons not intrinsically related to artistic development, the group began to dissolve, performing last in 1971.

This account may be old hat to poets who have been reading for years, but I concentrated on the stages of development for a reason. Obviously, at the end, we were moving into an area far more complex than the original "poetry reading"—if not theater, certainly something that was sophisticatedly theatrical.

The advantages of what we were doing over a traditional script were obvious. Whereas a play could, at times, seem wooden—tied to a particular story line and character conflict with well-rehearsed high-points and low-points—through poetry we could evoke a sense of immediacy and spontaneity that seemed to flow through the audience like a giant breath of fresh air. We could deal with the same themes any play might, with just as much depth. It was simply that poetry seemed to be a *way* of perceiving the themes that Black audiences understood. On a good night, a chain reaction fundamental to Black art was created; performer and audience could get the *call and response* going, like the great Black singers or the Baptist preachers. Is it theater? It is interesting that looking back on this experience, so many of us thought of BLKARTSOUTH as an "illegitimate" off-shoot of the FST. The underlying assumption was that theater ain't theater unless one can "mount the well-made play."

## As Unique to Our People as Blues & Jazz

Let's imagine we are entering Municipal Auditorium in New Orleans to hear Aretha Franklin. The auditorium, which sits where Congo Square once was, will be packed. Here in this auditorium, we will partake of an experience which transcends show biz or Aretha Franklin; for she is a modern conveyor of something so old and so basic that we don't know how old it is. Queen Aretha is the priestess of the religion of Black music. Before the night is over she will tell our story through music, through the magical instrument of the human voice, and set in motion the ritual of call and response, evoke from us and the entire audience a feeling that we are not merely *witnessing* a performance but are part of the performance; that the performance could not exist without us. We groove with the Queen who expresses in music what we somehow could never reduce to mere words; and somehow we realize that we don't really need to. Is it theater? Well, it certainly is *theatrical.* There is a bond of communication between performer and audience so strong, that if Aretha told us to fly off to the moon, we would as soon sprout wings.

Tomorrow morning, we might go out in the streets of New Orleans and see a parade led by a traditional band, say the Olympia. The sounds of the band evoke something old, something we cannot explain, something that, in the words of Danny Barker, "make an old woman hurting from arthritis, complaining incessantly of her aches & pains, her rheumatism, jump up and run out on the porch and do the bump and grind like she was eighteen years old." Hundreds of "second-liners" (dancers) follow the band, mostly Black youth. We discover they are headed for a park —the parade is to support a Black neighborhood demonstration against the eradication of the park. The people *need* the park. Is it theater? Well, let's put it like this: it is a performance, something these people understand, something they understand so well that hundreds of people who would never go to a neighborhood protest meeting are now there. Once there, they will listen. As at the auditorium, they themselves are essential to the function of the performance.

That afternoon and night we can hear the sounds of music echoing through the Black neighborhoods of the city, like talking drums, like the odors that float from many good pots, like voices speaking to each other in a language everyone who understands, understands. The Black neighborhoods of the city themselves are theater, a street theater-at-large. Black people use music for everything. Music expresses everything; music is the basis of our life theater.

Or let's take another example. We are listening to a performance by Sonia Sanchez, one of our great oral poets who came into maturity in the sixties. What the BLKARTSOUTH poets approached, she has mastered. As we listen to her connect her poems with a running monologue which explains the philosophical foundation of her work, she evokes the image of a great Baptist preacher. It is something we are used to. The genius of gospel, the Rev. James Cleveland, does the same thing when he performs. He has a different philosophical message, but we understand the form. We are impressed with the musicality of Sonia Sanchez's work. It is as if the basic conveyor of her ideas is music, an oral music through which her rhetoric is fused. She is singing to us, and we understand.

It is my conviction that as Black theater begins to reconceive itself, it must do so in terms of the oldest and most proven values of Black culture—our music, in all its forms—rhythm, dance, the oral tradition in its pre-American and post-American forms, call and response, spirituality, suggestiveness and subtlety of speech. It will not then be theater as we have known it in Western Europe or America. For instance, when we say *music*, we mean music not as a support, an accessory to theater, but a basic concept of *theater as music,* as another manifestation of music, another branch of music, another child of Black music. Music first, then rhetoric, then storyline. In the *Mwindo Epic,* the great mythical oral narrative of the Nyanga, Mr. Candi Rureke, the *She-Karisi* (the narrator) sings each section then narrates it. Theater as a form of music would not be very new, but very old and understandable to Black audiences.

The building on the foundation of oral poetry is an idea I feel obviously sound. We have suggested that Black poetry is musical, immediate, improvisational and is a natural form of Black art because of its origin in the African oral tradition. If we think of what we could now call the Black theatric as a *new* form based on old forms, the point of invention might center around how mime is used to further elucidate the fundamental themes established by music and poetry. We see an inventive use of mime in The Ballet Africaine. In their art, mime, dance, drums, and music all fuse to a peak of narrative and emotional excitement. The real work will take years of earnest experimentation, not abstract theories.

The question of form—how to make our new theater take its place as a functional black art—is most germane to southern groups because they *must* become functional or die, or they must live a half-life, a life confined only to western educated Blacks and liberal Whites. Given the genius for invention of our artists, we look forward to the time when the Black theatric can become as needed, as vital, and as strong as Black music.

# The Negro Ensemble Company:
# A Transcendent Vision

*by Ellen Foreman*

The 1960s stand out culturally as the most explosive decade in modern American life. No other period swept across the country with such a devastating tide of social, political and racial ferment. A shocked world witnessed the process of change in the entire social fabric of one of its most powerful nations. Deafening demands for a new America echoed in the highest political corridors in Washington and in the tiniest sharecropper's shack in Mississippi. Angry demands for a more just distribution of the country's economic wealth were translated into direct violent action: state troopers and citizens waged military warfare in the streets, often in the shadow cast by skyscraper corporation buildings. Psychologically and sociologically, volcanic forces erupted in a multiracial society which historically had never really understood the complexities of cultural pluralism. Ethnic minorities who had been murdered, exploited and despised for centuries reached for rifles and revolvers to settle ancestral grievances. It was Revolution in the etymological sense of the word: a turning around and over, a new circle. At the epicenter of that circle were Black Americans.

Deeply-buried sensitive nerves are laid open in any nation undergoing the turmoil of such an all-encompassing change. An ancient psychic wound is exposed. The communal soul of the people is in torment. Some hasty ill-conceived solutions were sought, but there were more thoughtful attempts to regenerate the lost soul of the nation. If the nation was spiritually tormented, a national mythology, a national religion, should have been available to provide comfort, for this is the purpose of human culture. However, pluralistic and multiracial New World America has never had any substantial, all-embracing national mythology or religion. The national soul, the national life, the national vision, has always been fragmented, racially, regionally and spiritually. In older traditional societies, such as Africa, Egypt, Greece, England, there would have been a unifying blanket of comfort. Often in these older cultures theatre has served this socially cohesive purpose, but America has never had a national theatre in this sense. Miraculously, however, as the movement for national change exploded in angry violence across the land, the Blacks, perhaps subconsciously recalling the structures of the older traditional culture which gave birth to them as a people, began to turn their eyes to the theatre. They used other arenas of combat, but some decided that their field of war would be in the oldest traditional form of communal protestation and expression known to humanity: a vibrant theatre, a living, breathing Black Theatre.

Many theatre groups began to bloom in Black communities in this period, but even heavy funding from government and foundation grants could not ensure their survival. Two such prominent groups in New York, Ed Bullins' and Robert Macbeth's New Lafayette Theatre, and Imamu Baraka's Black Arts Repertory, were short-lived, Baraka's collapsing after seven months. In both groups, ethnocentrism defined not only the audience addressed and admitted, but also the content of artistic expression. Black nationalist political philosophy offered too limited a perspective to ensure long-term existence.

What was needed was a broader vision. On August 8, 1966, in an article entitled "American Theatre: For Whites Only?" appearing on the front page of the *New York Times* Arts and Leisure Section, playwright Douglas Turner Ward proposed such a vision. He challenged the bourgeois parochialism of American theatre, questioning the very limited definition of the community served by the theatre, and cited the need for the creation of an autonomous professional Black theatre. His position reflected the Black nationalism of the sixties but also transcended it, and it was this larger vision that accounts for the continued, if difficult, survival of the Negro Ensemble Company into the late 1970s.

Black autonomy for Ward was not synonymous with racial separatism. He envisioned a theatre in which the Black playwright, "committed to examining the contours, contexts and depths of his experiences from an unfettered, imaginative Negro angle of vision," could communicate with an audience of "other Negroes, better informed through commonly shared experience to readily understand, debate, confirm or reject the truth or paucity of his creative explorations." The audience need not be all-Black, to the exclusion of Whites, but for the Black playwright Blacks were "his primary audience, the first persons of his address, potentially the most advanced, the most responsive, or most critical. Only through their initial and continuous participation can his intent and purpose be best perceived by others." Ward proposed a theatre "evolving, not out of negative need, but positive potential," and stressed the need for excellence. The plays would "concentrate primarily on themes of Negro life, but also be resilient enough to incorporate and interpret the best of world drama—whatever the source." What was most important was to establish a theatre of "permanence, continuity and consistency providing the necessary home base for the Negro artist to launch a campaign to win his ignored brothers and sisters as constant witnesses to his endeavors."

Ward's original proposal differed significantly from other Black theatre groups at the time in promising artistic freedom to the artist, in stressing artistic excellence, and in attempting to cultivate primarily Black audiences, without excluding Whites. The Ford Foundation, interested in Ward's ideas, asked him to submit a formal proposal. Six months later, a project that began as a three-man team effort was formalized into a professional company: The Negro Ensemble Company, with Robert Hooks as executive director, Gerald Krone as administrative director, and Douglas Turner Ward as artistic director. Their proposal combined an extensive training program designed to develop Black talent, with a fully professional theatre company. Four months later, with a Ford grant for $1,200,000, covering the first three years, NEC was ready to open its first season. A nucleus of talented actors, artists and musicians, many of whom would later become nationally and internationally famous, gathered in a typically ramshackle three-storey building sandwiched among cinemas, supermarkets, small restaurants and newsstands in New York's crowded Lower East Side. Among that first group were: Michael Schultz, Edward Burbridge, Marshall Williams, Bernard Johnson, Coleridge-Taylor Perkinson, Louis Johnston, Ed Cambridge, Rosalind Cash, David Downing, Arthur French, Moses Gunn, William Jay, Judyann Jonson, Denise Nicholas, Hattie Winston, Allie Woods, Esther Rolle and Frances Foster.

## *1967-1970*

Bold experimentation marked the early years. The new company could afford to take risks, and did, concentrating on developing a strong acting ensemble and gaining experience with a wide variety of styles. During the first season NEC produced four plays—three of them American premieres—by an international group of playwrights, all controversial. The first year made a strong statement of self-definition as theoretical ideas first expressed in the original vision took physical form. A "Negro angle of vision" was broadly defined, so that a play, *The Song of the Lusitanian Bogey,* written by a European about Portuguese oppression in Angola from the point of view of the oppressed, opened the season. The determination to remain "resilient enough to incorporate and interpret the best of world drama— whatever the source" was invoked in the transposition of an Australian setting in *The Summer of the Seventeenth Doll* to depict Black migrant workers in Louisiana.

Measured by audience response, the first season was an unqualified success. Crowds were turned away nightly for *Bogey,* two plays were returned for an extended summer engagement and went on tour in the fall, and the theatre began to attract a new audience, with racial ratio shifting from about 20% to about 60% Black in the first year. During this time NEC developed what was to be a permanent company and offered tuition-free workshops for Black performers and writers in voice, dance, and technical aspects of theatre. In April 1969, barely one year after its first presentation, NEC was awarded a "Tony"[1] for developing new talent and audiences.

The first year also brought abundant criticism, which was not unexpected. NEC was a pioneer, the first Black theatre of its

[1]The Antoinette Perry Awards are given annually by the League of New York Theatres for distinguished achievement in the professional theatre.

magnitude in America, and presented a glass house, open to responsible criticism and irresponsible target practice. Responses from White theatre critics on the major papers, varying with individual plays, were mostly supportive, but their reviews indicate confusion in their roles as theatre critics in evaluating Black drama. Subjective commentary on the inadvisability of what they perceived as segregated theatre and comments about their personal racial discomfort with the plays' content were common.[2]

Strongest and most sustained negative criticism came from parts of the Black community that Ward called "a few self-appointed defenders of the Black grail,"[3] and this too was to be expected. "Blackness" was measured by nationalist militancy, and NEC was perceived as not measuring up. The term "Negro" had already been discarded, defined politically as outworn Uncle Tomism. NEC, in choosing its name and resisting the pressure to change, was declaring its autonomy and defining its own terms. At the time, Ward defended the term "Negro" as having an honorable history. Recently, however, Ward admitted that although he clearly understood the implications of the change in terminology at the time, the pressure to change was not out of "principled reasons. It was a subterfuge, an attempt to impose their will on a foundling institution, an attempt to control it." Ward has never regretted his decision: "I would not be subject to vagrant pressures from wherever. Tactically, it was better to battle."[4]

Almost every decision the company made was challenged: their decision to locate downtown, instead of Harlem; their racial and ideological choices of plays and playwrights; their use of Whites in staff positions; their accepting money from the ultra-Establishment Ford Foundation. Peter Bailey, in an article entitled "Is the NEC Really Black Theatre?" answered with an uncompromising negative: for there is "no consistent philosophy of cultural nationalism directing the actions of its leaders."[5] Dick

---

[2]See Richard Watts, Jr., *New York Post,* January 3, 1968; Clive Barnes, *New York Times,* January 3, 1968; Martin Gottfried, *Women's Wear Daily,* December 18, 1968.

[3]Douglas Turner Ward, "Being Criticized Was To Be Expected...," *New York Times,* January 7, 1968.

[4]Personal interview, April 24, 1978. All other direct quotations by Mr. Ward were taken from this interview.

[5]Peter Bailey, "Is the Negro Ensemble Company *Really* Black Theatre?" *Negro Digest,* April 1968, pp. 16-19.

Campbell in *Negro Digest* accused NEC of being part of a conspiracy to keep Black people in the same place.[6] Later, in 1972, Paul Carter Harrison summarized the complaint of Black activists who felt that "there seems to be an attempt by the NEC to maintain a posture that will not be offensive to either the moderate or the activist."[7]

Ward was not disturbed so much by the content of the criticism as by the tone, "the rancor, venom, personal bias, subjective resentment and just plain old spite" which "practically cancelled out their usefulness as valid criticisms." As Ward remarked, "Six-figure money has a way of inflaming six-figure antagonisms."[8] Robert Hooks defended all of NEC's choices: "We are of Negro identity. We are doing plays concerning Negroes, about Negroes. If a good play is written by a green man from Mars and it fits into our season, we will do it."[9] More important, however, NEC was able to withstand the criticism and survive, forging its own multifaceted identity, at a time when other Black artists and institutions either withdrew from the hotbed of racial politics or succumbed to pressure.

The first three years presented drama of pan-African sweep: American, Caribbean and African perspectives, of astonishing range and quality, in a dazzling array of outlooks, moods and styles, offering the broadest possible definition of Black experience. Playwrights represented included Wole Soyinka, Richard Wright, Lonnie Elder III, Alice Childress, Ted Shine, Errol Hill, Ray McIver, Afolabi Ajayi.

## 1970-1972

Clenched fists against a background of African stone carvings suggesting an ancestral assertion of Blackness formed the poster design announcing NEC's fourth season: "Themes of Black Strug-

[6]Dick Campbell, "Is There a Conspiracy Against Black Playwrights?" *Negro Digest,* April 1968, pp. 11-15.

[7]Paul Carter Harrison, *The Drama of Nommo* (New York: Grove Press, 1972), p. 190.

[8]Ward, *New York Times,* January 7, 1968.

[9]"Robert Hooks and the Negro Ensemble Company." *Theatre Today* Vol. 1 No. 2 (Fall, 1968), p. 10.

gle." Black militancy was the theme of the first play, *Ododo,* a "musical odyssey" from Africa to the ghetto. Many professional critics saw this choice as a conscious shift in direction, a narrowing of the original vision, in order to pacify militant detractors and to attract a different audience. The imaginative range offered through the rest of the season, especially in the poetic expressionism of Derek Walcott's *Dream on Monkey Mountain,* a strong critical success that drew enthusiastic mixed audiences, belies that conclusion.

NEC continued in its second three-year period to offer diversity in perspective, in source, and in style, from the symbolic realism of John Scott's *Ride a Black Horse,* to the psychological domestic drama of Phillip Hayes Dean's *The Sty of the Blind Pig;* to the symbolic expressionism of Lennox Brown's *A Ballet Behind the Bridge;* to the documentary format of Arthur Burkhardt's *Frederick Douglass.* The 1972 season opened late, in December (a trend which has continued) with the one play of the season, Joseph Walker's *The River Niger.* Douglas Turner Ward directed and played the major role in the production. Luckily, it was a critical success and Ward made the decision to move it to Broadway where it ran for eight months and won the Tony Award for Best Play.

The trend was obvious and its root was financial. The initial Ford Foundation grant had run out after two and a half years, leaving NEC with a large deficit. For the second three-year period, Ford offered a matching grant arrangement: 3:1 for the first year, 2:1 the second, 1:1 the third. Federal, state and private grants did not make up the difference and NEC forfeited money it could not match. Internal organizational changes were made. Fred Garrett replaced Gerald Krone as administrative director, and Krone handled special programs. All decisions had to be made with money in mind. The theatre could no longer afford a resident company for it could not guarantee salaries. The "regulars" were kept "on call." The training program was sharply reduced and partially replaced by on-the-job training. In 1972, Ward admitted that it was becoming "financially unrealistic" to continue to operate at the program's former scope. He planned to put greater emphasis on workshops than on full productions, but he remained committed to developing new Black playwrights.

*The Great MacDaddy,* Paul Carter Harrison's folk-musical, blending traditional African story-telling and Afro-American oral tradition, was NEC's last "big" play, complete with original music, dancing, elaborate costume and set. Scheduled as the first play of the 1973 season, it didn't open until February 1974. It was, however, a box-office success, and it saved the season. NEC continued to present two new plays each season, all by Black American writers, tending toward realistic domestic drama, noticeably modest in cast size, set design and costuming, but still retaining high artistic quality. *The Last Breeze of Summer,* in which Douglas Turner Ward both acted and directed, another trend to become more pronounced as money grew scarce, did well, and was moved prematurely to Broadway at a time when general economic conditions were poor.

Artistic experimentation continued, however, in the satiric *Waiting for Mongo* by Silas Jones. *Eden,* Steve Carter's realistic drama depicting cultural conflicts between American Blacks and West Indians in New York in the twenties, opened new areas of dramatic content. One critic, praising the past few seasons at NEC, observed that "it is ironic that as the NEC has grown in artistic taste, so its financial support has weakened. For here it is, the first week in March, and the company only last night opened the first play of its season...."[10] More of the company's energy went into national and international touring and television productions. Benefit performances to raise money were staged frequently. Ticket prices were raised to a uniform $5.95, but could only account for ten to fifteen percent of the annual $500,000 budget.

In a recent interview Douglas Turner Ward talked candidly of NEC's critical financial situation and the total dependence of artistic accomplishment on financial resources. Artistically, he feels that the 1978 season has been the "most aggressive, most creative attack" he's ever waged, challenging audiences in new ways. Yet, even if he has a good play, he hasn't "a dime to put an

[10]Martin Gottfried, "Romeo and Juliet in Eden," *New York Post,* March 4, 1976.

ad in the paper, to let the public know we are there." The present is bleak financially; the future looks doubtful. Ward has applied to the National Endowment for the maximum production grant, financial aid to hire personnel to strengthen the corporate board internally and provide fund-raising expertise, and funds to create a laboratory program to pretest material in workshop readings. He feels it imperative also to reach out on a national scale, to introduce Black theatre in places where it has never been seen. He vows to "touch all bases" private and public for support, but recognizes that "Black is no longer 'in'" and that all arts institutions are in competition with one another. Despite the obstacles, or maybe because of them, Ward seems undaunted, as committed to experimentation and excellence, challenge and accomplishment as he ever was. Fully aware that there is an easier life, with lucrative commercial opportunities, Ward has not sold out, and retains a tenacious grasp on what is left of an institution struggling for financial survival.

Looking back over the record of the past eleven years, measuring NEC's achievements against its original goals, it is evident that this remarkable company despite its share of failures has overall been very successful. Its original artistic vision has been realized. A "Negro angle of vision" has projected over eleven years a total of sixty professional productions, thirty of them full-scale major productions with large casts of more than twenty. No other Black company over a consecutive period of eleven years has sustained such a sweeping range of dramatic forms: symbolic, realistic, expressionistic, poetic, folk, musical, historical, documentary, psychological, and sociological, a truly remarkable rainbow of aesthetic expressions. It is remarkable that even in 1978, in the face of its severest financial crisis with literally no money, NEC can still produce plays breaking new ground, deepening in its eleventh year its original vision. Gus Edwards' *The Offering* and Lennox Brown's *The Twilight Dinner,* according to Douglas Turner Ward himself, break new artistic ground for him and for Black Theatre generally. Their "Negro angle of vision" encompasses the universality of drama from a totally unselfconscious Black aesthetic. It is no surprise that Edwards was compared with Harold Pinter. The originality of his play found critics unprepared to deal with a growing Black aesthetic that started a decade ago.

From a Black vision has poured world drama, including the whole diaspora of Black expressions, from America, the Caribbean, and Africa. The multinational creative tides have arisen, rolling to and from the shores of the NEC. No White or Black company in the world can make this claim. Moreover, the artistic freedom of the Black playwright was never impinged upon in a decade of singularly dogmatic Black nationalist ideology—a striking human success. NEC has created a new theatre community by attracting, developing and educating a Black working-class and middle-class audience which did not exclude Whites. In so doing NEC reaches toward the possibility of a cultural redefinition of America.

From the point of view of sheer durability, NEC has been successful. Few noncommercial theatres, founded on a specific ethnic-aesthetic basis, last for eleven years and keep on going, surrounded by the jungle of New York's profit-oriented theatre: Broadway and multimillion-dollar musicals. The durability attests to the strength and intelligence of the original vision. Further, NEC has withstood the strongest test: racial criticism from its own Black community. It is ironic that some of its most public and acidic critics, racially, in the sixties would meekly ask privately to have plays produced. This racial endurance testifies to the immense human courage of people like Douglas Turner Ward, Steve Carter, Fred Garrett, and Gerald Krone, in addition to many Whites who have worked and are still working hard to keep this company in existence.

NEC's failures are a mixture of financial and administrative weaknesses. Their financial difficulties in part reflect the destructive American attitude toward art as part of the social fabric of civilization. The withdrawal of foundation funding reflects the questionable attitude of the White American power structure toward the just needs and demands of the country's Black citizens. But the current financial crisis also reflects the administrative failures of the NEC itself. No strong administrative structure was created to ensure successful financial footing. Douglas Turner Ward has tried to run a one-man show, and in this particular aspect, he has failed administratively. The middle period of branching into film and television reflects succumbing to easy temptation, a seduction possibly caused, in part, by the success of Joseph Papp of the New York Shakespeare Festival Public Theatre in launching financially successful Black plays. This NEC move was ill-considered. The film of *The River Niger* was a failure. The move to Broadway was also a lapse in NEC vision and goal, and further, showed lack of imagination and expertise in marketing successful dramas. NEC has failed to develop a permanent resident acting and directing company, an essential component implicit in the original vision. This lack is serious and inexcusable. The excuse that people left is not enough; they should have been encouraged and made to want to stay.

Over the last eleven years, the complexion of the Broadway theatre has changed. NEC has been influential in affecting that change by providing training and exposure to talented Black artists. But it would be an illusion to think that the professional theatre has opened up to Blacks. Rather, the visible change makes all the more apparent the enormous range of Black talent that had previously been neglected, and could be again. It would be a serious mistake to think of the NEC as merely a training ground that has served its purpose. The need for an autonomous, professional Black theatre, a "theatre of permanence, continuity and consistency," is insistent now, more than ever.

To conceive the original vision, to sustain it in the face of financial crises, weltering racial attacks, growing commercialism of surrounding theatres, devastating competition from million-dollar operations such as Joseph Papp's Public Theatre, and the new success of the banal Black musical says a lot about NEC. It also says something indefinably precious about Black art, Black Americans, Black people and Black theatre. The NEC has become, in image and in substance, the single national Black Theatre Company in America.

*The Negro Ensemble Company Productions, 1967-1978*

*1967-1968*

*Song of the Lusitanian Bogey* by Peter Weiss
*Summer of the Seventeenth Doll* by Ray Lawler
*Kongi's Harvest* by Wole Soyinka
*Daddy Goodness* by Richard Wright/Louis Sapin

Summer Repertory:
  *Song of the Lusitanian Bogey*
  *Daddy Goodness*
National Tour:
  *Song of the Lusitanian Bogey*
  *Daddy Goodness*

*1968-1969*

*God Is a (Guess What?)* by Ray McIver
*Ceremonies in Dark Old Men* by Lonnie Elder III
An Evening of One-Acts:
  *String* by Alice Childress
  *Contribution* by Ted Shine
  *Malcochon* by Derek Walcott
Workshop Festival
*Man Better Man* by Errol Hill
European Tour:
  World Theatre Season, London
  Premio Roma Festival, Rome

*1969-1970*

*The Harangues* by Joseph A. Walker
*Brotherhood* and *Day of Absence* by Douglas Turner Ward
*Akokowe* by Afolabi Ajayi
European Tour: Premio Roma Festival, Rome
World Theatre Season: London

*1970-1971*

*Ododo* by Joseph A. Walker and Dorothy A. Dinroe
Two One-Acts:
  *Perry's Mission* by Clarence Young III
  *Rosalie Pritchett* by Carlton and Barbara Molette
*The Dream on Monkey Mountain* by Derek Walcott
*Ride a Black Horse* by John Scott

*1971-1972*

*The Sty of the Blind Pig* by Phillip Hayes Dean
*A Ballet Behind the Bridge* by Lennox Brown
*Frederick Douglass,* through his own words by Arthur
  Burkhardt

*1972-1973*

*The River Niger* by Joseph A. Walker
*The River Niger* to Broadway
Repertory Workshop
Music and Dance Festival
Special Attractions Festival
Munich Olympics: "Cultural Session"

*1973-1974*

*The Great MacDaddy* by Paul Carter Harrison
*In the Deepest Part of Sleep* by Charles Fuller
National Tour: *The River Niger*

*1974-1975*

*The First Breeze of Summer* by Leslie Lee
*The First Breeze of Summer* to Broadway
*Waiting for Mongo* by Silas Jones
Television: *Ceremonies in Dark Old Men* — ABC

*1975-1976*

*Eden* by Steve Carter
*Livin' Fat* by Judi Ann Mason
Television: *The First Breeze of Summer* — NET
Adelaide Festival, Australia: *The Sty of the Blind Pig*

*1976-1977*

*The Brownsville Raid* by Charles Fuller
*The Great MacDaddy II* by Paul Carter Harrison
*Square Root of Soul* by Adolph Caesar
Virgin Islands Tour: *The Great MacDaddy*

*1977-1978*

*The Offering* by Gus Edwards
*Black Body Blues* by Gus Edwards
*The Twilight Dinner* by Lennox Brown

# The National Black Theatre:
# The Sun People of 125th Street

*by Jessica B. Harris*

It is difficult to write on the National Black Theatre for this theatre cannot be categorized. To categorize it would limit its function and hinder its performance. For the National Black Theatre is not just a theatre. It is much more. It is a "Temple of Liberation, designed to preserve, maintain and perpetuate the richness of the black life-style." This "temple" is partly formed by the resident acting company and liberation workshops, which are designed to promote positive black values. The workshops offer courses in evolutionary movement/dance, meditation, spiritual release; liberation theory and practice, numerology, astrology and ideology. Certainly, this is an indication that the scope of The National Black Theatre encompasses more than performance. Every Sunday, the theatre gives a symposium in which they present major artists, thinkers and scholars to the Harlem community.

A major goal of the company is the creation and perpetuation of a black art standard. Barbara Ann Teer, the company's spiritual force and prime mover, reasons: "You cannot have a theatre without an ideology, without a base from which all of the forms must emanate and call it Black, for it will be the same as Western theatre, conventional theatre, safe theatre." The National Black Theatre has evolved its own black art standard. It states:

> Our art standard requires that all theatrical presentations, be they dramatic plays, musicals, rituals, revivals, etc., must:

"The National Black Theatre: The Sun People of 125th Street" by Jessica B. Harris. From *The Drama Review,* Vol. 16, No. 4 (T-56, December 1972), pp. 39-45. Reprinted by permission of *The Drama Review* and the author.

1) *Raise the level of consciousness* through liberating the spirits and strengthening the minds of its people.

2) *Be political,* i.e., must deal in a positive manner with the existing conditions of oppression.

3) In some ways *educate,* i.e., "educate to bring out that which is already within." Give knowledge and truth.

4) *Clarify issues,* i.e., enlighten the participants as to why so many negative conditions and images exist in their community in order to eliminate the negative condition and strengthen the positive condition.

5) Lastly, it must *entertain.*

From this statement we know that the National Black Theatre is not a "downtown" group whose notion of black theatre is white theatre in blackface. This theatre is setting up new priorities and new criteria for judgment. They are creating a new art from the black cultural experience in America and Africa. As Ms. Teer states: "when one is sincerely interested in dealing with the roots of blackness and of the black life-style, it is impossible to deal with those roots without dealing with Africa."

The National Black Theatre and the Temple of Liberation, an institution for a black nation, were founded in 1968 by Ms. Teer. She decided to form her own theatre after a variety of experiences as an actress and director. Her training was basically European: she studied at the Wigman School. She does not like to approach theatre on a commercial plane. When she started to perform on Broadway and in off-Broadway productions, she found that the frame of reference of most of the actors was entirely different from her own.

The National Black Theatre has largely eliminated the negative dog-eat-dog aspect of Western theatre. This has been accomplished through an essentially black medium: the black family structure. The tradition of the black family unit has been strong; anthropologists and sociologists have written tomes on it. Ms. Teer took the concept of the black family unit and extended it to the members of her company. As members of the same family, the negative aspects of Western theatre are virtually eliminated for the performers as they each have areas of specialization, as well as freedom to experiment. Sound technicians act. Actors build sets. Lighting people dance. There is total cooperation in all phases of her theatre.

The first year of the theatre's existence was largely experimental: there were no public performances; workshops and symposiums were scheduled each week. The thrust of the theatre was determined in this first year of experimentation. The National Black Theatre concluded that black people were a spiritual people, an energy people, a sun people. The vibrations put out were so heavy that at one symposium a brother got up and asked if the group would baptize his child. Now that's spiritual! This spirituality provides the force and energy that is at the basis of all of the theatre's performances.

The National Black Theatre does not consider entertainment its overriding goal. Its major goal is to re-educate, to restore spirituality and a cultural tradition that has been stripped from blacks in America. This is called consciousness-raising by some. The theatre's performances—characterized as either rituals or revivals, not plays—deal with situations that are relevant to the members of the Harlem community. The group attempts and usually succeeds in providing the largely Harlem spectators with new information about themselves, so that they leave uplifted, reaffirmed, enlightened.

Music is a big part of the lives of most black people. It is also an integral part of the performances at Ms. Teer's theatre, as is dance and movement. The music and movement are thought of in the African sense and are integrated within the performance, flowing naturally out of the situation that is being presented.

The major innovation of the performing company of the National Black Theatre is the creation of a black theory of acting and liberating. As the black experience in America is quite different from the white one, black actors are frequently asked to play roles that have nothing to do with the basic reality of their lives. This may seem to be a contradiction but Stanislavski's "as if" does not always work for black actors in these times. With the theories established by the National Black Theatre, the black actor can return to himself, to his culture, to his heritage and to his people.

As this technique requires a liberation of self and an eventual liberating of others, the actors at the National Black Theatre are not called actors but liberators. They must go through a process of "decrudin" in order to find whatever is at their base as individuals. This "decrudin" process is a purification that is undertaken not only by the actors but, in a small way, by the spectators, too. This is a more spiritual base than Western tradition permits and is perhaps only possible because the group is such a close-knit family organization.

What is the process that creates the new black actor? It is the spiritual base of The National Black Theatre. It is to this base that the actors return in order to find the primary force for the theatre. Most black people in the world are united by a common tradition of worship that cuts across social classes and national differences. This is not a common religion but rather a similarity of worship that can be traced through the religions of Africa to those of the Caribbean and finally to the Pentecostal and "Holy Roller" churches in the United States. It is from this energy that the National Black Theatre works to create a liberator.

The first exercise that is given at the theatre's workshop is to go to a church and a bar; not St. Patrick's Cathedral and a swinging singles bar, but rather the churches and the bars that are the psychological centers of the Harlem community. From the observations that the student liberator makes in these two places and in the subsequent places that he is assigned to visit, he begins to build his own interpretations of the Five Cycles of Evolution. The Five Cycles of Evolution are at the base of the technique of the actors of the National Black Theatre. They are:

    I—The Nigger
    II—The Negro
    III—The Militant
    IV—The Nationalist
    V—The Revolutionary

Ms. Teer evolved the cycles, the labels. They are divided in terms of degrees of qualities, or values. The liberator must find the most salient and significant characteristics of each cycle and use these for theatrical purposes. The cycles are not limiting; they are a base to work from. They are an expanding thing and they cannot be taken strictly at face value for then they become one-dimensional. They must be taken as guidelines so that they become all-encompassing and as such offer an open area in which the liberator can work. In the analysis of the character type, the liberator is encouraged to deal with the type in terms of colors, music, values and other indications of the life-style that he is representing. Each year the student-liberator is encouraged as a final project to create a workbook using clippings, music, and swatches of material to illustrate the five cycles. The workbook presents a constantly changing picture of the cycles to the company. For the cycles, seemingly static, are in a constant state of change. This can be attested to by walking through the streets of any black community; the creativity of the black mind is constantly at work. For example, what the "Nigger" might have been wearing last year is definitely out this year. The notebooks insure that the National Black Theatre is constantly revising its material. They enable the group to be always "on the case" and therefore more relevant to the Harlem community.

But what do the cycles represent? Ms. Teer explained them to Charlie Russell (writer-in-residence) for an article that appeared in *Essence:*

> *The Nigger* is the most free, colorful and creative character. But he has strong materialistic and individualistic values.
>
> *The Negro* is also individualistic and materialistic. He accepts white cultural standards and is an imitation of a white American imitating Europeans, imitating Romans, imitating Greeks, who we all know were imitating Africans.
>
> *The Militant* is an aware *Nigger,* still individualistic and materialistic. He's in that I-hate-all-white-people bag but he's not for real change, and is only angry and frustrated because the system won't let him in.
>
> *The Nationalist* is non-materialistic. He is intellectually for the collective. This is the first step into true blackness, where you develop a consciousness and a love for your people.
>
> *The Revolutionary* is the highest, the most evolved of all the cycles, for in this cycle you deal with the spirituality of blackness. You know who you are, what you have to do, and you simply go about quietly doing it.

Although the cycles may seem excessively political, the National Black Theatre is not simply using revolutionary rhetoric. They are changes, internal changes that are necessary before the external ones can take place.

The Five Cycles of Evolution are at the basis of the rituals and revivals presented at the National Black Theatre. All of the characters are representative of the people of the Harlem community. The characters can move either up or down the vertical standard of the five cycles. In most cases, the progress is positive, for Ms. Teer's theatre is about nation building.

The National Black Theatre recently sent a questionnaire to the people of Harlem, asking them how they felt about being black and how their feelings on this subject had changed in the last few years. This information should make the work of the group, both as a performing company and as an agent of nation-building, more relevant to the community.

The ideas being implemented at Ms. Teer's theatre have had repercussions: many other black theatres are turning to Africa for inspiration and looking for a spiritual base. The National Black Theatre has that kind of power.

## *A Revival! Change! Love! Organize!*

We begin with a combination of spiritual and human sources: Africa/Harlem, Oshun/Junkies. The cultural diversity of the black American life-style comes spilling out onto the stage in the person of fire dancers, a dope pusher, a whore, and a priestess. The space is divided into two areas.

The first part of the action takes place in a Harlem street, much like any other street, perhaps 125th Street, the location of The National Black Theatre, or like the street in *Ain't Supposed to Die a Natural Death*. This street, however, is not seen through the fourth wall of a proscenium arch; you are on it, in it. It is all-encompassing, all-embracing. As you enter the theatre space the characters greet you, embrace you, confront you, affront you. They are all there: the Sunday sisters going to church; the Saturday night brothers coming home from the bars; whores selling "feels"; a basketball hustler who will exchange shots with you; a drunk panhandling with a sign on his back "My mother has sclerosis"; a junkie selling underwear for his next fix — all the characters on the streets in any black community. All the Five Cycles of Evolution are represented.

In the second space—where the second part of the performance takes place—there is an atmosphere of calm and tranquility. There are subtle colors and joyous sounds. This is the Temple of Liberation. The two different spaces could be symbolic of the two extremes of the Five Cycles of Evolution. The "home" of the "Nigger" is the street in much the same way as the "home" of the "Revolutionary" is the Temple of Liberation. It is interesting to note that the places/spaces are united; each one needs the other. To get from the "street" into the temple you've got to go under a heavy chain, in much the same way that in order to become a revolutionary you've got to go through the "decrudin" process.

The audience is always a part of the performance. The liberators are constantly speaking to and with them, moving them. In both spaces, spectators are seated around the outside of a central, essentially open, acting space—an approximation of the theatre-in-the-round form. The actors at times sit with the audience, and the spectators in turn play ball, dance, drink, and eat with the actors. The interchange is total. No restrictions are placed on either group. This type of action happens more in the street space than within the temple.

The two spaces are linked by a storyline that was created by Charlie Russell (writer-in-residence of the group) with the aid of Barbara Ann Teer, the director of the group. The plot deals with the destruction of the Harlem community by drugs. It exhorts black people to begin to support other black people and to encourage positive values. This all takes place with an almost revivalist fervor, though the title, *Revival,* has nothing to do with down-home camp meetings. This is definitely a didactic work, but then the major aim of the National Black Theatre is education and nation-building.

As you enter the first space, the liberators casually show you to a seat and talk to you about various things, or try to panhandle, or dance. This continues until the main story begins: Porky, a junkie, owes money to Walt, a pusher, but he has lost the money and cannot pay. He resorts to stealing a woman's wallet but is caught. So he has no way to return the money that he owes Walt. When Walt comes to town, he threatens Porky and gives him a short time to come up with the money. This is the essence of the first part of the play. This action takes place in the street setting.

In his flight from Walt, Porky has been befriended by Toussaint, who is the leader of the Temple of Liberation. Toussaint invites all the liberators and spectators to attend a revival later in the evening. This action is juxtaposed with the descent of the goddess Oshun, Yoruba goddess of love. Oshun sees what has happened to her children, sees the state of the community, and exhorts all to unify and to love each other. The descent of Oshun is the occasion for a scene of possession taken from the voodoo rites of Haiti and is one of the highpoints of the first part of the performance. Another highpoint is a fire dance that marks the entrance of the Kabakas, who present the revival in the second part of the performance.

The intermission—a concession to traditional theatrical practices—is marked by a continued mixing of the liberators and the audience. Snow-cones are given out, plus drinks and food. The actors circulate, talking and joking with the audience. At the end of the intermission, the spectators are told that the time has come for the revival and that they should get ready for it. A wall of the space is then rolled back, and the spectators are ushered under a heavy chain and into the Temple of Liberation.

The atmosphere of the temple is completely different from that of the street. It is spiritual and not worldly. Most of the spectators are surprised to see the characters from the first part of the piece in the temple. But the plot continues. The first few minutes in the temple are spent introducing the Kabakas, the Liberators, and ourselves. Information gleaned from a book tells the spectators that blacks form only 11 percent of the population of the United States but that they drink more than 49 percent of the scotch consumed in the country and 25 percent of the grape soda; they spend 200-million dollars on suits and 8-million dollars on ties. The Kabakas feed the audience this information and then tell the spectators that blacks have money and power as consumers and that they should use this power to support black institutions —not only the Temple of Liberation but all black institutions. The audience becomes so caught up in this that when the plot continues—Walt breaks into the temple to look for Porky—it seems to be an intrusion. Yet the plot must continue. Walt takes Porky from the temple. The revival continues.

Some time later, Porky is returned to the temple, but he has been brutally beaten by Walt. This is the occasion for a scene of healing in the manner of the faith-healing evangelists. Toussaint, the leader of the Kabakas, heals Porky and implores him not to go back to dope and the life of the streets but rather to become a spiritual being and to work for positive black change. Positive black change: That is the message not only to Porky but to the entire audience, and on that note the play ends.

After the play, the actors, still in character, go around and thank the members of the audience for coming and ask them to tell their friends about the play because the National Black Theatre is a low-budget, no-budget group. It depends on the community for support. In an atmosphere of unification, the play lets out, the audience going out into the street—a street much like the street in the play. Good-byes are said to people who only a few hours before were perfect strangers. The revival has worked its charm. The unifying force of the National Black Theatre has begun to do its work.

*The Participators: Audiences and Critics*

# Into Nationalism, Out of Parochialism

*by Larry Neal*

We will scream and cry, murder, run through the streets
in agony, if it means more soul will be moved, moved to
actual life understanding of what the world is, and what it
ought to be. We are preaching virtue and feeling, and a
natural sense of the self in the world. All men live in the
world, and it ought to be a place for them to live.

IMAMU BARAKA

It took a long time for the idea of nationalism and the making
of black theater to come together. The nationalists of the twenties
—the back-to-Africa and separate-states movements—didn't
have any understanding of, or interest in, cultural activities. For
example, something in Garvey's Jamaican colonial background
had left him in awe of European culture; even the uniforms of the
United Negro Improvement Association looked like imitations
of a bizarre Austro-Hungarian guard troupe. The depth of Garvey's misunderstanding is vividly illustrated in a description
from Harold Cruse's *Crisis of the Negro Intellectual:*

> Garvey held a mass meeting at Carnegie Hall, in downtown New
> York City. It was packed to overflowing; white people attended too,
> as it was well advertised in white newspapers.... Items on the
> musical part of the program were: Ethel Clarke, Soprano, singing
> Eckert's "Swiss Song" and Cavello's "Chanson Mimi"; The Black
> Star Line Band, in smart uniforms, rendering overtures from
> *Rigoletto* and *Mirello;* the New York Local Choir, fully robed,

"Into Nationalism, Out of Parochialism" by Larry Neal. From *Performance,*
Volume I, No. 2 (April 1972), pp. 32-40. Reprinted by permission of the author
and the New York Shakespeare Festival Public Theatre.

singing the "Bridal Chorus" from *The Rose Maiden* and the
"Gloria" from Mozart's 12th Mass; the "Perfect Harmony Four" in
the Sextette from *Lucia;* Basso Packer Ramsay sang Handel's "Hear
me ye Winds and Waves." The second half of the program were
speeches by the Officers and [Garvey]. Subjects were: "The future
of the black and white races, and the building of the Negro nation."

However, the idea of a theater which would address itself specifically to Afro-American socio-cultural reality is not new; it appeared, in a non-nationalist context, in a 1927 essay, "The Negro
and the American Theater," by Alain Locke:

> In the appraisal of the possible contribution of the Negro to the
> American theater, there are those who find the greatest promise in
> the rising drama of Negro life. Others see possibilities of a deeper,
> though subtler influence upon what is after all more vital, the tech-
> nical aspects of the arts of the theater. Until very recently the
> Negro influence upon American drama has been negligible, where-
> as even under the handicaps of second-hand exploitation and re-
> striction to the popular amusement stage, the Negro actor has
> already considerably influenced our stage and its art. One would
> do well to imagine what might happen if the art of the Negro actor
> should really become artistically lifted and liberated. Transpose
> the possible resources of Negro song and dance and pantomime to
> the serious stage, envisage an American drama under the galva-
> nizing stimulus of a rich transfusion of essential folk-arts and you
> may anticipate what I mean.

This statement is "integrationist," but important. Alain Locke was
one of the major forces of the Harlem Renaissance. He had to
come to grips with theater and other forms of popular entertainment, because it was in this sphere that the image of the Negro
had been most vilified: thus Harlem Renaissance aesthetics
called for an art which was a more human reflection of Negro
life. By 1927, Negro theater had had some notable successes to
its credit, and shows like *Shuffle Along* and *Blackbirds* had a
profound influence on Broadway theatrical form, which absorbed
and modified — what we'd now call "co-opted" — black singing and
dancing style.

In the same period, Zora Neale Hurston, an anthropologist
and folklorist, made an important contribution through her work
on Afro-American folk culture: blues, spirituals, gospel singing,
dance patterns in Jamaican life, the ritual forms that spring from

Haitian voodoo. She wanted to develop "a truly Negro theater," whose speech patterns, visual structure, and movements were clearly rooted in Afro-American folkways. But she had no ideology of blackness in mind at all; she was oriented towards being a part of the American system, and was, at the most, an unconscious cultural nationalist. Hurston thought Garvey was a buffoon; she even wrote an unpublished satire on his organization.

The black theater of the thirties was an off-shoot of the Federal Writers Project. Its orientation was essentially Marxist, and its concerns those of the Communist Party; it was integrationist and had no independent ideology. However, in 1937 Richard Wright wrote an essay, "The Blueprint for Negro Writing," laying out an ideological and aesthetic orientation for the black writer, and combining a nationalistic thrust with thirties leftism. He discusses the development of a specifically black life, and in that sense the essay is the beginning of black cultural ideology, of the idea of "blackness."

Communist influence on Negro theater held sway into the forties, modified into liberalism during the fifties, and reached its apotheosis with Lorraine Hansberry's *A Raisin in the Sun. Raisin in the Sun* was, aesthetically, a competent play in the realist/naturalist tradition. Ideologically, it was the embodiment of the liberal integrationism which dominated the black political struggle of the mid-fifties and early sixties. Martin Duberman's *In White America,* Ossie Davis' *Purlie Victorious,* and James Baldwin's *Blues for Mister Charlie* are all various aspects of the liberal consciousness that found its active expression in the non-violent civil rights movement.

Yet it's in that movement we find the beginning of what's now known as black theater. The Free Southern Theater was first organized as the cultural wing of COFO (Council of Federated Organizations, the overall grouping of southern civil rights organizations), by people actively engaged in SNCC [the Students' Non-Violent Coordinating Committee] : Len Holt, Gil Moses, and John O'Neal. It was activist theater: they wanted from the start to do plays "written for a Negro audience, which related to the problems within the Negro himself and within the Negro community." The FST ended up facing all the difficulties that have confronted black theater people in the past eight or ten years. Their public statements were part Marxist, part nationalist,

but *Waiting for Godot* was one of the FST's first main productions—to say the least, an apparently odd play for an activist
theater. Yet it wasn't unusual in SNCC, in 1964, to find organizers
who were existentialists under the influence of Camus, who
leaned towards a theater of the absurd—a theater essentially
turned on itself. What's more, the FST, while directed *toward*
the black community, was co-directed *by* white theater people,
co-acted by white northern professional actors, and entirely fi-
nanced by whites. As the movement changed, with the end of
non-violence and the beginning of Black Power, the FST evolved
with it and is now an exemplary activist black community theater.
But though it first began and then reflected the course of black
theater, its influence in the North was small.

It was LeRoi Jones' *Dutchman* that radically reordered the internal structure of black theater, first of all by opening up its
linguistic range and breaking with the social realism which
dominated the forties and fifties, and second (more important
and in spite of vague allusions to the theater of Artaud and the
absurdists) through the decidedly utilitarian strategy which informs the play—it is implicitly but very clearly addressed to the
radical sector of black socio-political consciousness. After *Dutchman,* Jones created the Black Arts Theater in Harlem, 1965, from
which sprang Black Arts West and a multitude of other theaters
on its basic model: a theater in the community, and a manifesto
for the theater as a total nationalist institution, a reflection in
miniature of the entire nation, which was meant above all to be an
instrument for the raising of political, ethical, and aesthetic consciousness. The Black Arts Theater believed in political activity
on the part of its company members. They held classes in nationalist political theory and black history; Harold Cruse taught
there for a while.

The ideology of blackness sprang out of American blacks'
legitimate need to develop a philosophical orientation which
would let them find some space within themselves to move, a
private space that set them apart from whites, from the European
value system. It was also a reaction to a racist language and
imagery that had made blackness a thing of evil; it is analogous
to the ideology of negritude shaped by Sékou Touré and Aimé
Césaire and to the self-realization movements developed in the
Caribbean. It's a frame which finally provided operational iden-

tity to black artists. Because this ideology was primarily created out of psychological need, it has no single text. The word "black" is the key to all its meanings, but sometimes black stands for spiritual commitment to black people; sometimes it means establishing a natural relationship with one's own culture; sometimes it has religious connotations (you don't need Christ, find your blackness instead). When one person says of another, "he's a Negro, he's not black," all these meanings overlap. And it's these meanings which are involved, and intertwined, in the search for a "black" form.

Throughout the sixties, many black artists and intellectuals engaged the question of a "black aesthetic" through Afro-American music. The blues singer, the jazz musician, and the show business entertainer were seen as secular extensions of the ritual first shaped in the church service, out of the songs and movements brought from Africa. That's why Ellison describes Bessie Smith as a "priestess," a "celebrant"—the same thing can be said for Aretha Franklin, Ray Charles, John Coltrane, Duke Ellington. Music was considered an instrument of truth, the "purest expression" of the black reality in America; Sun Ra attempted to construct a cosmology around it. And writers lamented the fact that literary expression was incapable of having the same effect on black people as music. From the point of view of craft, the central problem confronting the black playwright is that play craft involves procedures that are cognitively different from those of music. But that didn't prevent black literary artists from trying to make some kind of aesthetic link between literature and music. In poetry, for example, the emphasis was on oral delivery and some poets formed ensembles much on the order of rhythm 'n' blues groups.

The nationalist ideology, with its philosophical trappings, when added to this stress on musical structure, was responsible for the development of new ritual forms, while the overtly political and social aspect of black thinking led to a parallel reliance on naturalistic forms—Ed Bullins is now called the "new O'Neill" by the *Times*. Barbara Ann Teer of the National Black Theater, for example, moved away from the crafted play and toward a ritualist theater. (The only crafted play ever performed by the NBT was Charlie Russell's *Five On the Black Hand Side*. And it wasn't done in Harlem, but at the American Place Theater.)

Teer came into the black theater after a considerable amount of work on the off-Broadway and Broadway stage. At first, she emphasized the development of the black actor through a training technique that would be an organic extension of Black life styles. Exercises were done against the background of black music. One series of improvisational exercises arose out of a blues modality, and was called the "Nigger Cycle," another set was accompanied by the music of John Coltrane, and was referred to as the "Righteous Cycle"—I recall this was the "highest cycle." Each cycle below the cycle of righteousness contained negative as well as positive elements. Elimination of the negative elements—European values, bourgeois attitudes, self-destructive tendencies—was called "decrudification," i.e., a particular kind of psychic purgation. Teer's pieces are big, with many performers, and she uses her work in a functional manner—at the Congress of African People last year, she opened up one of the sessions by moving her whole brightly costumed troupe into a huge auditorium, carrying red, black, and green flags, singing, chanting, dancing down the aisles. Her texts for the rituals are unimportant and corny, but her company's energy is extraordinary—proved by the fact that they played the Apollo Theater, successfully.

You never could put one of Robert MacBeth's New Lafayette rituals in the Apollo. The New Lafayette rituals are, for me (and such reactions are very personal) failures, failures of energy. Their modality is oriental, characterized by silence and darkness. (I haven't seen the last one, which I understand has African drumming and dancing.) They tend to be slow, plodding, studious, and done with a very solemn air. Pieces open in a darkened theater, perhaps to symbolize a plunge into the inner self. An off-stage voice lays down the text, which is too long, and too mysterious. The only reason to stress all this is that when ideology is removed from the rhythms and vigor of the people on whom it is based, it becomes self-defeating and cannot be made into meaningful images and gestures.

I'd like to mention one other specific group in contrast to the NBT and the New Lafayette which, working in Harlem, a nationalist community, have had to be nationalist and separatist or lose contact with their milieu: the Negro Ensemble Company never announced itself in the same terms as these other black theaters. It is located in the East Village. When the NBT and the New

Lafayette discouraged white critical attention, the NEC welcomed it, and functioned among other things as a link between black community theater and white American theater. The nationalist reaction a few years ago was strong, and hostile; Imamu Baraka referred to the NEC company as "Negro Theater Pimps":

> They are square on the definition. Negroes who have been blown up to prominence (actually, the founders, and movers, etc., less than second rate talents who because of their lack of skill can play tagalong to white arts, but also continue the dead myth of black inferiority...because most of them *are* inferior, if you can dig it... that's why Whitey pushes them) because of their commitments to white desires rather than black needs....

Pretty harsh, and somewhat exaggerated. Most NEC productions are highly polished, and the group is one of the few which presents a wide variety of black theater. It's too bad they're downtown; the presence of such a theater in the black community would have far reaching effects; particularly now that the extreme separatism of the other theaters is being reevaluated. A black critic is expected to attack all playwrights working, and all theaters playing, anywhere outside the black community, but I don't think that's necessary. The NEC just represents another tendency within the movement. It wants to be accepted off-Broadway, wants to be accepted by critics, and honestly says so. Everybody else wants the same thing but doesn't want to admit it. (When the New Lafayette, for example, got bad reviews from white critics they stopped white critics from coming to the theater. Now Eric Bentley gives them a good review of *Psychic Pretenders* in the *Times,* and in my *mail* comes a copy of Bentley's review sent by the New Lafayette Theater!) The NEC advertises plays in newspapers, their thing is in the open, they want to be accepted as theater in the same way other theaters are accepted. In other words, their ideology is that of the civil rights movement.

In the sixties, the idea spread uptown that whites contaminate the theater, and one reason for this was that some blacks had gotten tired of entertaining white people, of being part of the Negro's image as someone who made his money playing to white folks. Another reason was the feeling that blacks needed a theater where they could be themselves without being spied on; a kind of psychic withdrawal from whatever might harm a group's spiritual integrity, into a self which didn't have to be expressed in opposition to white people. It was a protective move.

Now that black artists are surer of themselves I think the New Lafayette has taken the right course, one which other black community-based theaters will follow. It is trying to break away from parochialism (and parochialism meant fear). They want to get the works of their playwrights done everywhere they can be done. This year [1972—Ed.] two New Lafayette playwrights have had their plays produced, by the Public Theater and by Lincoln Center: They are making *forays* out to other institutions but maintain their base. Our theater should challenge the establishment theater; black artists must confront western art, not withdraw from it. Remember how black sound dominates the American musical sensibility. Part of what we should do now is take on the American theater sensibility and replace it with ours. Or, at least, place our statement in the arena.

Already, our development has led to the emergence of a clear community orientation toward black artists and toward art as a means of discovering the essential issues of our existence. For the first time many black people are aware that something is happening vis-à-vis art that relates to them and that they can partake of on a serious level. For example, my mother has been going to the theater, and not because she's my mother. She is straight-out working-class, but she and her friends go to plays in search of some kind of fundamental understanding about the texture of life: her life, and life in general. An ideological artist can speak to a community who understands his vocabulary; before the black arts movement, and the linking of nationalist politics with art, there never was an organic relationship between the community and the black artist, except singers and jazz musicians. The new acceptance of art has had an important effect on consciousness, on attitudes toward oneself, and, above all, on that level of aspiration which is necessary for any ideology of change. When you present a horizon, you can show the need for change, and build a model for what change should be.

# It's a Long Way to St. Louis:
# Notes on the Audience for Black Drama

*by Adam David Miller*

As we examine a play, we can experience the playwright grappling with such questions as: Who am I? Who are these characters I people my world with? What is my world? *Who am I creating it for?* The play, that most public, most social of the arts, is created for an audience, and it is this question of audience, more than any other single question, that has bedeviled this country's Negro playwrights.

James Weldon Johnson thought the question not one of a single audience but rather one of audiences. In "The Dilemma of the Negro Author" he wrote:

> ...the Aframerican author faces a special problem which the plain American author knows nothing about—the problem of the double audience. It is more than a double audience; it is a divided audience, an audience made up of two elements with differing and often opposite points of view. His audience is always both white America and black America. The moment a Negro writer takes up his pen or sits down to his typewriter, he is immediately called upon to solve, consciously or *unconsciously,* this problem of the double audience. To whom shall he address himself, to his own black group or to white America? *Many a Negro writer has fallen down, as it were, between these two stools.*[1] (emphasis added).

"It's a Long Way to St. Louis: Notes on the Audience for Black Drama" by Adam David Miller. From *The Drama Review,* Vol. 12, No. 4 (T-40, Summer 1968), pp. 147-50. Reprinted by permission of *The Drama Review* and the author.

[1] *The American Mercury,* December, 1928, p. 477.

Johnson's white audience, though ignorant of Negro experience, had nonetheless hard-to-change preconceptions about what Negro experience was and how it wanted to see it presented; it demanded that the Negro playwright lie about his experience. Since most white playwrights up to Johnson's time had defined Negro life in a way that enabled their white audiences to feel superior to Negroes, thus contributing to the view of Negroes as objects rather than subjects, most whites were willing to see Negroes presented only in images that permitted white comfort. While Johnson's black audience would permit a "real" Negro to be shown in a "Harlem," with all his foibles and faults—all his humanness—they would object to this same Negro on Broadway. For Broadway and the eyes of whites, certain subjects and manners dear to the hearts of Negroes were taboo. To Broadway the Negro audience wanted only a *nice* Negro to be shown. So, to please either audience, the Aframerican playwright had to cut a stencil and fill it in with whichever viciousness or banality he imagined one or the other of his audiences conceived. This was a real dilemma.

Johnson considered for a moment the idea of the Negro author saying: "Damn the white audience! ... What I have written, I have written. I hope you'll be interested and like it. If not, I can't help it." But only for a moment. These words were hardly written when he acknowledged: "But it is impossible for a sane American Negro to write with total disregard for nine-tenths of the people of the United States. Situated as his own race is amidst and amongst them, their influence is irresistible."[2] Thus 40 years ago, in the infancy of black playwrighting, Johnson was able to predict with accuracy that our best playwrights would, often unconsciously, vitiate their creative energies by diverting their attention to a white audience that was often hostile, ignorant, deaf, and blind.

What Johnson might have said but didn't was that the white audience could act as cultural tyrant partly because white society apparently offered great rewards to those authors whose creations fitted within socially acceptable limits, rewards the non-white society could not match. All of the cultural apparatus, publishing, radio, film, was under the control of whites, and if the Aframerican writer wanted to continue the recognition he had begun to receive, he had better toe the line.

As long as the black playwright himself sought the rewards

[2]*Ibid.*, pp. 480-81.

held out by the white society, he had his characters seek them, with the result that most of the work done was less a frontal attack on the society as evil than on certain evils of the society. Such a playwright felt and showed in his work that if only certain evils, such as racial discrimination and segregation, were removed, then he and other blacks could take their "rightful places" alongside whites.

Even such a playwright as Langston Hughes—who knew his proper subject matter, who proclaimed at the beginning of his career his rejection of the self-denying "urge to whiteness" and was proud to use his "racial individuality"[3] —was an integrationist at his core, and felt that the society could be changed so that whites and Negroes could live side by side in harmony. The Hughes statement went something like this: "You are mistaken about me. I am a better man than you think, give me the chance to prove it. Once you understand this, we can work together to create a better world for both of us." Hughes was essentially an optimist about the society and about its potential for change.

Because of what he was saying, Hughes needed a white audience to say it to, despite the fact that the lives of his characters were little understood by that audience; indeed, they were little understood by those "literate" Aframericans who felt they had nothing in common with the *poor* blacks making up Hughes' fictive world.

The racial values that make up Lorraine Hansberry's fictive world also could make sense only if projected to a white or white-seeking audience. The virtues of the Younger women in *A Raisin in the Sun*—thrift, caution, hard work, good sense—contrast with the lack of these virtues in the men. Walter Younger attempted to make a quick killing, and in the process lost the family's savings to a black con-man. The women want to leave the black ghetto. To do this they attempt to buy a house in an all-white district. When the whites try to buy them out, Walter is willing, but the women convince him that it is in the interest of his manhood to insist on a fulfillment of the deal. The Youngers have the viability of their black lives destroyed but are denied the white life they seek. They are being forced to measure their lives by the standards set by their oppressors. This, of course, is senseless for

[3]Langston, Hughes, "The Negro Artist and the Racial Mountain," *The Nation,* June 23, 1926.

Negroes. In short, Miss Hansberry is saying to a white audience: here are the Youngers, a good American family operating in the tradition of thrift and hard work, the trademark of successful mobility in the society. They only want a chance to prove to you what good neighbors they can be. Why don't you let them?

James Baldwin bases his *Blues for Mister Charlie* on the murder of Emmet Till, a young Negro boy, by at least two Mississippi white men. In the play the murderers become one man, and it is the psyche of this man Baldwin presents for his audience's understanding. To explain his effort, Baldwin writes:

> ...we have the duty to try to understand this wretched man; and while we probably cannot hope to liberate him, begin working toward the liberation of his children. For we, the American people, have created him, he is our servant; it is we who put the cattle prodder in his hands, and we are responsible for the crimes that he commits. It is we who have locked him in the prison of his color. It is we who have persuaded him that Negroes are worthless human beings. ...[4]

In these "Notes" Baldwin addressed himself to what appears to be an *American* audience, that is, the entire body politic of the country. But his words trip him up. When we look closely, we see that they could not possibly have been meant for Negroes. How could he ask Negroes to be responsible for white crimes? By what twisted logic could he expect Negroes to see themselves *causing* white violence and oppression?

And the play itself, about the murderer's trial and the events preceding, poses questions for whites, not for Negroes, to answer. Nor is the asking of them likely to help a Negro audience "understand this wretched man." Besides, it is not the duty of the Negro to understand this man. It is the duty of a white audience to understand him and his duty to understand himself. Too often Negroes have been offered the job of civilizing whites; it is high time whites began civilizing themselves. It is the duty of the black audience to understand itself, and the duty of the black playwright to help in this understanding.

Even the comic playwrights fall into the trap of either catering to the good will of a white audience, or of making statements

---

[4] James Baldwin, "Notes for Blues," *Blues for Mister Charlie* (New York: Dial Press, 1964), p. xiv.

irrelevant to Negroes. Young white Cotchipee of Ossie Davis' *Purlie Victorious* becomes the first member of Big Bethel, the church the Negroes wrestle away from his father. He is happy to join, they are happy to have him. In Douglas Turner Ward's *Day of Absence*, we see a black audience laughing at the whites in their helplessness at the loss of their Negroes for a day. Look, they say, the white folks need us. Ha, ha. One must ask if this is something Negroes need to be told. The image of the black woman who raises Miss Ann's children at the sacrifice of her own is one all too familiar to Negroes. What Negroes need to know is not that they are needed by whites but that they are needed by one another. They need to be shown by their playwrights how to reach out to each other across this need.

There are, fortunately, playwrights who do address their work to Negro audiences. Ed Bullins' *How Do You Do* speaks to the middle-class white-seeking Negro, who was the despair of Langston Hughes. Bullins' *Clara's Ole Man* gives the ghetto Negro a picture of life that is "just around the corner" or perhaps the block. Marvin X's *Take Care of Business* shows a young black's determination to try to understand his children as he was unable to understand his father. Dorothy Ahmad's play [*Papa's Daughter*] shows a young girl helping her father see that she is his daughter, not his wife. (LeRoi Jones should belong here, but despite his brilliance, he is still trying to do something with whites, either flagellating them verbally, or parading them as beasts. The results are often vivid but shallow abstractions.) These are plays about Negroes addressed to Negroes. They provide characters blacks can identify with. They speak to the black experience in ways blacks can understand.

To return to James Weldon Johnson. Johnson felt the Negro author could solve the dilemma of the divided audience by "standing on his racial foundation,...fashion something that rises above race, and reaches into the universal in truth and beauty."[5] Johnson here is buying a particularly limited idea of "universal." The Negro playwright must reach the "universal" *through* race. He should write in such a way that he makes sense to his Negro audience. If this playwright addresses himself to the needs of his Aframerican audience, their need for an under-

[5]*The American Mercury*, December, 1928, p. 481.

# The Black Theatre Audience

*by Thomas D. Pawley*

For as long as I can remember, theatre directors in Black colleges have been complaining about the behavior of student audiences. Students have been described as gauche, vulgar, impolite, naive, and childish. This evaluation is shared by some students, particularly those involved in dramatic productions. That there is some justification for this appraisal will soon become evident. Even the advent of Black theatre with its concern for Black people has not materially changed behavioral patterns. In fact, it has intensified certain responses. For example, at a recent production of *Ceremonies in Dark Old Men* at Lincoln University of Missouri, the actor playing Blue Haven exclaimed following a performance, "Doc, did you hear that cat on the front row? He talked all through my long speech. He was actually competing with me. I felt like telling him to shut his goddam mouth." An exasperated director in Alabama once stopped a production to lecture the audience on its behavior. There have been moments when I have thought of giving up the theatre because of my distress over audience reactions.

Although my concern is the college audience, I suspect these behavior patterns are to some extent characteristic also of Black audiences in high schools and in community and professional theatre. According to Doris Abramson, "Brooks Atkinson... would sometimes review the audience when he went to a Harlem theatre commenting on their *childish delight* [Italics mine. Is this the old stereotype?] or their appreciation of lines beyond his

"The Black Theatre Audience" by Thomas D. Pawley. From *Players,* Vol. 46, No. 6 (August-September 1971), pp. 257-61. Reprinted by permission of Byron Schaffer, Jr., editor of *Players.*

comprehension."[1] And Loften Mitchell records in *Black Drama* the occasion when Jules Bledsoe was performing *The Emperor Jones* in a Harlem theatre and was admonished by a member of the audience, "Man, you come on outa that jungle. This is Harlem."[2] Further confirmation of my belief came in February, 1971, when I attended a production of the Pulitzer Prize play *No Place to Be Somebody* at the Studebaker Theatre in Chicago. The reactions of adult Blacks who constituted a considerable proportion of this commercial audience were hardly distinguishable from those of college students and were on this occasion a source of distraction to many in the audience, although the actors seemed unperturbed.

The main complaint seems to center around the distracting nature of certain responses which are ill-timed, unpredictable, and apparently unrelated to the mood or action of a scene, thus frustrating both the actors and a considerable portion of the audience. No one charges the students with a failure to enjoy or appreciate the plays per se but, say the directors, the enjoyment and appreciation are often misplaced and misdirected. To be specific: "They laugh at the wrong time," or "They make a comedy out of everything," or "You never know what they'll laugh at." It is true that laughter seems to be a major response, even in serious drama and tragedy. However, the comments of directors are in themselves interesting since the laughter may point to the recognition of inherent weaknesses in acting or directing or to the perception of incongruities, anachronisms or subtleties by the Black student audience.

In any case, with efforts being made to build Black theatre, the establishment of Black Studies departments on so-called "white" college campuses, and the increasing demand by students for Black Theatre on these campuses, it might be well to describe this student behavior more specifically, to analyze its causes and to suggest ways of controlling it without destroying its spontaneous exuberance and enthusiasm.[3]

---

[1]Abramson, Doris, *Negro Playwrights in the Professional Theatre*, Columbia University Press, New York, 1969, p. 186.

[2]Mitchell, Loften, *Black Drama*, Hawthorne Books, Inc., New York, 1967, p. 84.

[3]Cf. Reardon, William R., and Thomas D. Pawley, eds., *The Black Teacher and the Dramatic Arts*, The Negro Universities Press, Westport, Conn., 1970.

Student behavior patterns may be placed into two categories: the non-verbal and the verbal. Non-verbal responses may be further subdivided into vocal and physical reactions. To the former belong shouting, jeering, hooting, laughter, and an infinite number of non-linguistic vocal reactions indicative of approval or disapproval, enjoyment or dissatisfaction. Physical responses include beating on the seats, stamping on the floor, nudging or kicking companions, clapping or slapping hands ("give me some skin"), rocking back and forth, and, in extreme instances, spontaneously leaping to one's feet in the manner of a sports crowd. Such responses are basically emotional, automatic and non-reflective. (I do not exclude the possibility, however, that some may be the result of cerebral activity.)

Verbal responses, as in the anecdote cited earlier, involve talking aloud sometimes to the actor, sometimes to the audience, sometimes to one's self, and sometimes to nobody in particular. It may come as the audience anticipates the action at an emotional crisis, as an expression of approval or disapproval, as an attempt to enlighten less perceptive persons as to "what's happening," to forewarn the audience, especially if the individual has seen the play before, or as a spontaneous verbal response, e.g., "Right on, brother!"

I recall at a production of an original play of mine, *F.F.V.*, several years ago, when the light-skinned Negro doctor is about to learn at the end of the play that, unknowingly, he may have married a white woman, a student said aloud, "Yea, Jim. If he was shook up before wait until she tells him what's happening. He'll be tore up!" Here was a positive indication of deep involvement in the play and a keen perception on the part of the student which had to be verbalized.

The net effect of these responses on the audience may be summarized in part as follows:

1. Actors and directors are frequently upset, depressed, and angered.

2. Listening is made more difficult, thus vexing a considerable portion of the audience.

3. Whites in the audience are variously perplexed, amazed, confused, and amused.

4. Blacks are embarrassed and apologetic in mixed audiences
when they constitute a minority and angered or annoyed when it
is predominantly Black.

Believing as I do that the first step in controlling behavior is
to discover causes, I wish now to suggest those portions of a play
which may stimulate these reactions or overreactions. It may be
noted from the foregoing discussion that many of these are pre-
dictable and typical of all audiences. It is only in the degree of
response that the Black student may be atypical, and then, only if
he is being compared to white middle-class behavior patterns.

What elements within the play or in its production bring on
the reactions I have been describing?

Ranking high among the stimuli is the language or dialogue
of the play. Swearing, especially if it involves the "dozens,"[4]
sexual references, both the overt and covert, sharp repartee, and
"flams,"[5] will undoubtedly produce whoops of delight. Scenes
of violence and physical conflict will also arouse the audience.
A realistically staged fight between a drunken old woman and
her grandson in a recent production of Ted Shine's *Morning
Noon and Night* caused many in the audience to leap to their feet
when she slammed him to the floor. A resounding slap brought
exclamations and comments. In a production of LeRoi Jones'
*The Salve,* one student yelled, "Shoot him again to make sure
he's dead!"[6]

Love scenes, especially bedroom scenes, as for example that in
*Ceremonies in Dark Old Men,* when the "Old Man" attempts to
seduce the young girl, or that between the Black sailor and the
English girl in *A Taste of Honey,* have set the audience to
murmuring.

The costuming of the play itself may bring spontaneous vocal
reactions. Period costuming has produced gales of laughter,
especially if it reveals skinny legs or ungainly physiques. Form-
revealing or skimpy dresses have produced wolf whistles, expressions of approval, and, in some cases, what amounts to an open
request for a date. In our production of *Dutchman,* one aroused
student yelled at the actor playing Clay, "If you don't want her

[4]Insulting references to one's parents, especially the mother.
[5]Any remark which downgrades another person.
[6]This may also have involved vicarious participation in the physical punish-
ment of a white man. Cf. Mitchell, *loc. cit.,* pp. 102-103 for another example.

————, I'll take her." Audience reactions to a sheer and form-revealing kimona worn by a steatopygic actress in a production of *Mooney's Kids Don't Cry* actually brought the performance to a momentary halt.

Recognition of acquaintances in an unfamiliar role may lead to heckling, applause and laughter. If the behavior is at variance with the actor's reputation on campus, so much the worse, e.g., a notoriously poor student playing a scholar or a reputed homosexual making love. Here the individual's personal reputation creates negative empathy and prevents emotional identification. Again, a well-known student may have a personal following or a claque who applaud his every move. A corollary to the above is recognition of the familiar in any form. If it is a familiar song the audience may begin rocking with the music.

Music of and by itself, particularly "soul music," has a potent effect on the audience. An effective rendition of *Jesus Is My Rock*, sung in gospel style in Ted Shine's play, brought spontaneous applause for the performance itself. Poorly sung, the response might have been equally strong but negative.

The critical judgment of the audience is aroused by any form of atypical behavior. A poorly played love scene, fight scene, argument, etc., may bring laughter or murmurs of disgust. The converse is just as likely to bring resounding applause. Strange or eccentric behavior, such as that of Amanda Wingfield in *The Glass Menagerie* shouting, "Rise and shine," or "operating" on the gentleman caller, prompted such statements as, "Ain't she crazy" and "Look at that silly woman." If the behavior or language is in contradiction to what the character is or what the audience feels the character should do or be, its disgust or disapproval may be vocalized, e.g., a young man trying to seduce a girl and affirming that he loves her when the audience knows he does not, or a doting mother begging her grown son not to leave her for his young wife.

Responses which are particularly vexing to a great many actors, directors, and at least some of the audience, occur during serious moments and for no apparent reason. The curtain line in *Hedda Gabler,* when Judge Brack responds to Hedda's suicide with, "People don't do such things," brought whoops of laughter. I later discovered that the audience was enjoying the judge's discomfiture rather than Hedda's death. This tendency to laugh at the serious first came to my attention in a segregated movie theatre many years ago during the film *King of Kings.* I was enthralled, as was most of the audience, during a scene from the Old Testament depicting the Flood. The mood was broken, however, when a man shouted, "Lord, look at that water running up the hill." How could anyone refrain from laughing after that?

After 30 years of observing Black college audiences all over the South and Border States, I have reached certain conclusions concerning the causes of the behavior I have been describing. In all honesty, I must admit that the reactions have been to the traditional dramatic literature, classical, Elizabethan, modern and contemporary. But in recent years, similar responses have been induced by productions of *A Raisin in the Sun, Day of Absence, Tiger, Tiger Burning Bright, Ceremonies in Dark Old Men, Dutchman* and *The Slave,* plays concerned with the Black experience. I wish now to suggest some probable sources of this behavior. What follows is subjective and perhaps needs to be examined more closely by social and behavioral scientists.

The traditions of the Black church have to some degree determined and conditioned the responses of a majority of Black college students—perhaps more than any other factor. Its relaxed, open, democratic atmosphere has encouraged the maximum verbal and physical participation long before "living theatre" was conceived. By Black church, I mean those religious institutions founded, organized, controlled and attended exclusively by Black people.

Responses range from the emotional frenzy generated by the sanctified churches, which sometimes causes emotional and physical prostration, to the restrained "amens" of deacons and elders in the conventional Protestant churches. Ministers deliberately set out to arouse their audiences. A failure to do so may mean a negative reaction to the sermon and/or a poor collection. James Weldon Johnson has immortalized this preacher in *God's Trombones,* and William Pipes has skillfully analyzed his techniques in *Say Amen, Brother!* Black churches are steeped in the oral traditions of folk cultures brought over from Africa, preserved through slavery and adapted and modified to the exigencies of the Christian faith.

While there is no uniform pattern, we will find the following responses in varying degrees within the church:

Verbal, e.g., (1) Talking to the preacher, (2) Testifying, (3) Shouting.

Non-verbal exclamations and shouts.

Physical reactions, e.g., clapping, stamping of feet.

Direct participation, e.g., walking to the front to deposit money, spontaneous group singing.

In summary, a general lack of emotional and physical restraint encourages a wide variety of verbal, non-verbal and physical responses, leading to direct participation in the church service. These become powerful factors in conditioning the Black student's reactions in the theatre since they begin very early in life.

Patterns of behavior developed in the nightclub, entertainment-stage syndrome within the Black community also begin very early. Musicians, singers, dancers, and comedians who served their apprenticeship in the ghetto night spots of Kansas City, Chicago or Harlem, or in stage performances for mass audiences, have grown accustomed to the close interplay, the give-and-take between audience and performer. The same lack of restraint, lack of inhibition, and the participatory impulse inherent in the church has characterized these audiences from time immemorial. I do not include here the heckling which occurs in most nightclub situations but a spontaneous rapport which serves as an incentive to the artist to perform at the highest level.

At stage performances, audiences may sometimes dance in the aisles or join the musicians on the stage. Distinctive solo renditions bring spontaneous and prolonged applause and shouts of approval. From the advent of institutionalized racial segregation at the turn of the century, Black people gave mass support to Black performers at the Regal in Chicago, the Apollo in New York and the Howard in D.C. I submit that the patterns of behavior at these theatres and in the nightclubs have carried over into the legitimate theatre experience and conditioned student reactions.

Still another factor determining the student behavior is the sports crowd psychology. Since Jackie Robinson broke the color barrier in major league baseball in 1947, Black people have been attending professional sports events in increasingly large numbers. Historically, they have always supported the Black athlete just as they did the Black performer when this was possible, as, for example, Joe Louis during the Thirties. This support prior to World War II was focused on the Black high schools and colleges: the Vashon-Sumner contests in St. Louis, the Wilberforce-Tuskegee football game in Chicago, and the Howard-Lincoln game in Atlantic City. This support was extended also to segregated professional baseball and basketball. I once attended a Black all-star baseball game in Chicago at Comiskey Park with an attendance of 50,000 when Satchel Paige was in his prime. And the New York Renaissance Cagers were attracting huge crowds long before Abe Saperstein organized the Harlem Globetrotters.

For at least 50 years, therefore, the behavior patterns of the sports crowd at boxing, baseball, basketball, and football, with its exuberance, boisterousness, beer and whiskey drinking, have been a part of the Black experience. In essence, the response of this crowd is to applaud and cheer what it likes and to boo or jeer what it does not like. Vestiges of this sports crowd behavior undoubtedly carry over into the legitimate theatre experience.

Ranking high among the causative factors is the absence of a legitimate theatre-going tradition with a consequent lack of knowledge of "traditional" behavior patterns. With the demise of such groups as the famous Lafayette Players and the touring road company generally during the Twenties and Thirties, and the advent of, first, the movies, then television, as primary sources of drama, the overwhelming majority of Black people have been denied the live theatre experience. They, like the greater portion of the American public, have become dependent upon electronic media for their dramatic fare. One may sit in the movies and munch candy or peanuts or smoke; one may sip coffee or a cocktail, and comment aloud as he watches T.V. in the privacy of his home—behavior patterns which until recently were not tolerated in Western legitimate theatres. Dinner theatres may change this.

The Black middle class has never been devoted to the theatre. Black community theatres are few and far between, and poorly supported. Too few Black people have attended the dozen or so Black colleges which have significant theatre programs for this to have had any appreciable effect on theatre-going habits, and at white colleges a Black face in the audience is the exception rather than the rule. Few Black high schools have developed the kind of [drama] program comparable to those in athletics and music so that the exposure to live theatre has been minimal among both high school and college graduates.

I am sure that even those inclined to attend the theatre were sometimes stymied by the economics of the Black community from making the trip downtown; or perhaps the middle-class setting and behavior patterns in the theatre, in contrast to those of the nightclub or stadium, have been prohibitive factors rather than the price of the ticket.

Hopefully, the rise of the Black Theatre movement will change all of this and establish a theatre-going tradition. Meanwhile, when one is in a strange or unfamiliar setting, and is ignorant of behavior patterns, he will either inhibit his normal reaction patterns or act as he always has in similar situations.

As a corollary observation, the theatre assumes a certain level of language facility and familiarity with dramatic literature on the part of audiences. That is to say, a certain level of knowledge and education. This is perhaps one reason why Black playwrights are using the language of the ghetto in their attempt to build Black theatre—a language which is immediately perceived and understood.

The great emphasis on remedial education among Black colleges attests to the inadequacy of language skills (reading, writing, speaking and listening), all of which are necessary to the fullest enjoyment of traditional drama. Thus the college theatre becomes a continuing training ground, perennially facing the problem of controlling audience response.

Finally, I wish to suggest that laughter, one of the principal responses of student audiences, may have become a subconscious reaction to both the tragic and the comic, developed as a result of the exigencies of the Black experience in America. Black people were forced for more than 300 years to hide their real feelings, to disguise their real thoughts, to present an outward appearance of joy and equanimity. Laughter thus became the device for deceiving the "man" and sublimating frustrations. The result, of course, was the creation of the myth of a happy-go-lucky, naive darky incapable of perceiving the niceties of Western culture.

On the other hand, student laughter may be a highly developed tool for indicating the perception of incongruities. I am sure that in many individuals it is a consciously used device for indicating both appreciation and disapproval. I would also be less than honest if I did not admit that, in a considerable number, it is a spontaneous response to that which is foreign to their experience and, therefore, in their eyes, ludicrous. I have observed that, as the student audience grows more sophisticated, laughter decreases. Also, when Blacks are a minority their reaction is indistinguishable from whites. It's almost as if they are afraid to laugh. But in an all Black audience, the laughter response is typical in varying degrees of both Black Ph.D.'s and bus boys.

What then are the implications of the behavior I have been describing?

Fundamentally, I believe the responses are an indication of enjoyment, that they are a measure of the extent of the audience's involvement, and that audiences are not consciously being disruptive. To put it another way, the audience appreciates and frequently likes what it is seeing. An absence of these responses may be an indication of an unfavorable reaction. This was my distinct impression at recent performances of Ionesco's *The Chairs* and *The Lesson,* which not only were poorly attended by Black students at Lincoln University but also did not induce (someone said, "Thank God!") the usual responses. On the other hand, the more sophisticated Blacks and whites were genuinely pleased, even commending the students for the exemplary behavior. My impression was simply that they did not "dig" Ionesco.

There are other implications. Directors must begin to deal directly with audience behavior, anticipating the typical responses, preparing their actors for them, and attempting to minimize those reactions which are clearly out of place by various techniques which are available.

Senior and junior high schools with predominantly Black student bodies must begin to develop significant curricula, as well as extra-curricular programs, so that Black youngsters will not perennially enter college in swaddling clothes because of this cultural deprivation. Black colleges must provide the widest possible theatrical experiences (no less than 12 productions over a four-year period) so that students may close the gap in this aspect of their education. Audience training must necessarily become a part of the educational theatre experience in both high school and college, and it should begin in the high school.

From my reading of theatre history, I have concluded that Black college audiences are not unlike those who viewed the plays of Plautus and Shakespeare, especially the latter. Elizabethan audiences were among the most exuberant in the 3000-year history of the theatre. Shakespeare and his fellow playwrights provided them with processionals, sword fights, low comedy scenes, long rhetorical speeches, ghosts and murders in very earthy language, as well as the poignant moments, such as that which evokes the magnificent poetry of Macbeth when he learns that his wife is dead.

A recent news item from Africa suggests that Black audiences may have unconsciously preserved a cultural trait. The following appeared in the Washington *Post* of January 4, 1971, in a dispatch from Lagos, Nigeria:

> Duro Ladipo is a leading Nigerian playwright, who would rank somewhere among Neil Simon, Arthur Miller and Zero Mostel in American theatrical terms. Nigerian companies often feature the playwright in the lead, and his wives, cousins and friends pitch in as well.
>
> Ladipo played the king in his folk opera entitled, *Moremi, the hine of Ife.* The costuming was rich and extravagant, like an English period piece. Thematically, the play, constructed on Yoruba myths, resembled ancient Greek drama.
>
> But the most overwhelming part of the evening for a foreigner there was the audience. Between explosions of laughter, spectators offered a constant stream of suggestions, instant criticism and jokes of their own as Ladipo's company continued its performance. Surprisingly, the injections and other symptoms of the Yoruba affinity for anarchy did not seem to hamper the players, who were able to build much of the byplay into their production.

Herein may be the ultimate solution in controlling the Black college audiences: innovative playwrights, like the Elizabethans, who write for a particular audience, and creative actors who, like the artists of the *commedia dell'arte,* are masters of improvisation and byplay.

# Critics, Standards and Black Theatre

*by Margaret B. Wilkerson*

There is a war in progress between Blacks and whites over the nature of reality. And the battle lines are clearly drawn in theatre. Black artists have told white critics that they are not qualified to judge Black theatre because they have neither the frame of reference nor the necessary experience. Black directors have denounced critics for various reasons. One director whose multi-racial casting policy was severely attacked asserted that critics are hampered by their preconceptions about theatre. Another stated that these influential individuals discourage fledgling actors and writers by judging workshop efforts as fully realized productions. Others have considered barring the press from their productions, while one angry director offered to break the fingers of critics when they even think of reviewing a Black production.

Hatred for critics is not new nor unique to Black artists. Joseph Papp, producer of the New York Shakespeare Festival Public Theatre, has quarrelled with some of the best-known reviewers. However, the disenchantment of Black artists with white critics is rooted in the conviction that these critics lack the cultural sensitivity to evaluate their productions. As Black drama critic Clayton Riley has written: "Those who willingly chose to ignore what we were about until recently are hardly the ones to tell us what forms our craft and our artistic concerns should take, particularly since their silence and indifference were fundamental contributors to the exclusion of Blacks from America's cultural marketplace for so long."[1]

When theatre critics turn their attention to Black theatre, they

"Critics, Standards and Black Theatre" by Margaret B. Wilkerson. This article appears for the first time in this volume. Reprinted by permission of the author.

[1]*New York Times,* Sunday, June 14, 1970.

are inclined to apply the same standards that they use with white theatres, and frequently begin by dismissing most Black productions as social rather than artistic, as parochial rather than universal. Martin Gottfried claimed that "the white public condescends to it [Black theatre] and the Black public is lured on by its primitively parochial level."[2] William Drummond, in reviewing *Angela Is Happening!*, a play about Angela Davis which was presented at the Inner City Cultural Center in Los Angeles, said that the evening "was more like an encounter group than theatre," and noted that "the fine line between make-believe and reality was lost by the audience for an uncomfortable moment."[3] Beneath the condescension implicit in these statements is a more fundamental conflict over the definition of theatre. Rather than quote charge and counter-charge, this essay will explore the nature of this conflict and propose new parameters for the criticism of Black theatre.

Points of criticism often turn on this basic question: What is theatre? Is it event, process, ritual or all of these? What is the role of audience? The critics in question seem to limit theatre to those few hours in which the finished production is performed on stage, that is, to the space of time allotted to the single performance which they see. All process preceding those moments and any consequences of those moments in the lives of the audience are ignored, unless some action such as an actors' fight or an audience riot rises to a level of sensationalism sufficient to pique their interest. The role of audience, the handling of subject matter, choice of language, viability of artistic forms and many other considerations hinge on the critic's expectations of theatre.

The history of criticism offers few answers. In fact, the conflicting theories seem to suggest how *not* to approach theatre, the critic's personal preference often being the only consistent factor. While personal taste, when admitted and examined, can be a useful touchstone for a reviewer, a critical approach should begin with an understanding of the nature of the theatrical event as well as a knowledge of the raw materials basic to that particular theatre's cultural context. Just as a present-day critic's knowledge

[2]Martin Gottfried, "Is All Black Theater Beautiful? No," *New York Times,* Sunday, June 7, 1970.

[3]William Drummond, " 'Angela' Played as a Courtroom Drama," *Los Angeles Times,* March 3, 1971.

of script, history and style generally forms a background against which he or she judges Shakespearean or other works, so a fair evaluation of Black productions requires an understanding of Afro-American history and culture and an acknowledgement of Black theatrical expectations. The ever-present oppression which separates Blacks from whites and the highly charged emotional atmosphere which informs that condition make it particularly difficult for a white critic to share a Black artist's perspective. What is the nature of the theatrical event for Black people? It is at once communal, functional and participatory. Productions which feature Black casts in plays relating to their lives have an instant community—not spectators, but a spiritual community. The audience rarely needs Coleridge's admonition to "suspend disbelief" because the emotional distancing is not present. The mirror of self that the performance provides is rare in this society which expects Blacks to filter their self-perceptions through stereotyped images in films and television or through a blind identification with white characters. Perhaps for that reason Black audiences are as likely to applaud or cheer a *statement* with which they agree as to acknowledge a performer's craft. The emphasis on the former is not a lack of taste, but a recognition of theatre as metaphor and dramatic action as a functional extension of their lives. For them the theatrical event is not an objet d'art but exists as effective tool of personal and social development. Anthropologist Janheinz Jahn finds the same tendency in West African culture:

> Beauty is identified with quality, above all with effective force. . . . The European [sees] the "work" as an object *having* meaning and rhythm. But the African sees the poem as recited, the carving in its function as stimulus in the worship of an orisha, the mask in the movement of the dance. Art . . . is in Africa a force, and the force is accordingly the essential not of the art-object, but of the exercise of art. Art in Africa is never a thing but always an attitude or activity. . . .
>
> African philosophy stands consistently on the side of the artist; for it the finished work as it stands in the museum has nothing more to do with art; it is a "thing," it is wood, vocable, lead, ivory, glass, colour—nothing more. It is not the artistic product that is impor-

tant in Africaṇ philosophy, but the fashion in which the creative, form-giving process takes effect.[4]

Although contemporary African-Americans are centuries removed from their tribal forbears, their history and sensibility have conspired to retain the theatrical or performance event as effective force.

In some ways, this view of art begins to account for the Black audience's response to theatre. For many, the theatre is similar to the Black church and serves the historical function of a place where Black people can be in the majority, away from the scrutiny or imposition of outsiders. Here they can drop the many pretenses adopted for survival and "let it all hang out," participating in a heightened reality. This relationship of audience to performance has persisted, despite the form, style or location of the theatre. Mainstream theatre sometimes dictates containment and control to an audience: the separation of audience from performers, the written text of the play which discourages improvisation, and other elements make many European-American productions fixed events whose form, down to the last detail, is frozen in rehearsal. Although there are Afro-American plays and productions which have copied these forms, Black audiences have not copied their white counterparts, but have maintained the tradition of participation, the lively intercourse with and vocal response to the performance. This phenomenon is not dependent upon location or social class. It occurs in the store-front theatre, in the sophisticated metropolitan house, even in the auditoriums of the university campus.

Many Black theatres of the 1960s and 1970s are abandoning the concept of theatre as an isolated art form and are consciously developing a theatre which relates intimately to the desires and needs of its community in many and varied ways. Triumph amidst adversity, the dangers of narcotic addiction, the joy and struggle of male/female relationships, the spiritual poverty of assimilationism are only a few of the themes being explored in these community theatres. There are significant experiments which tap African culture for viable combinations of music,

[4]Janheinz Jahn, *Muntu: The New African Culture,* Grove Press, Inc., 1961, pp. 173-174.

dance, mime and storytelling. These artists are responding to the clarion call of LeRoi Jones (Amiri Baraka) who declared that theatre must force change and *be* change. The words of Ed Bullins inform their work:

> We don't want to have a higher form of white art in black-face. We are working towards something entirely different and new that encompasses the soul and spirit of Black people, and that represents the whole experience of our being here in this oppressive land. We are attempting to take all the things that are positive in us, our music, our very strong religious expression, our own life style, and incorporate them into our art on a collective basis. Our aim is not only to become better artists, individually and collectively, but to create a uniform positive art.[5]

Critics who approach these efforts with too many preconceptions about the nature of theatre apply standards which these artists do not respect, which they do not seek to achieve.

What standards, then, are relevant? The critic must begin with simple respect for the work of Black artists. For example, Gilbert Moses, prominent Black director, complimented John Lahr on his review of *The Duplex:* "He talked about the repetition of characters in *20th Century Cycle*. He knows about Ed Bullins. He's interested in Bullins. He can take a character from *In New England Winter* and see the progression through *The Duplex*. To me, it means he respects Bullins as an artist. The fact that the criticism has this awareness gives it so much more weight. He has a basis for criticizing besides opinion."[6]

Black theatre should be taken on its own terms and judged by its own objectives—as should any theatre. Because these productions answer to a different cultural downbeat, the critic who is outside or on the parameters of that cultural experience, should approach judgment with humility. Perhaps then the universal or humanistic elements of Black theatre could pierce the cultural biases of the critic. Too many critics discuss Black theatre as if it were unrelated to their own lives. The theatre offers a unique opportunity to step into the space of other individuals and other

[5]Marvin X, "Interview with Ed Bullins," in *New Plays from the Black Theatre,* Bantam Books, Inc., 1969, p. xii.

[6]Bill Eddy, "4 Directors on Criticism," *The Drama Review,* Vol. 18, No. 3 (T-63), September, 1974, p. 27.

experiences—with *safety*. To ignore this chance is to treasure ignorance.

Addison Gayle, Jr., editor of *The Black Aesthetic,* provides an important reference point for understanding the terms and expectations of Black theatre:

> A critical methodology has no relevance to the black community unless it aids men in becoming better than they are. Such an element has been sorely lacking in the critical canons handed down from the academics by the Aristotelian Critics, the Practical Critics, the Formalistic Critics, and the New Critics. Each has this in common: it aims to evaluate the work of art in terms of *its* beauty and not in terms of the transformation from ugliness to beauty that the work of art demands from its audience.
>
> The question for the black critic today is not how beautiful is a melody, a play, a poem, or a novel, but how much more beautiful has the poem, melody, play, or novel made the life of a single black man?[7]

The Los Angeles Black theatres of the last decade were established to make life "more beautiful" for Blacks in Los Angeles after the Watts Revolt of 1965. That upheaval, which left thirty-three Blacks dead, stimulated artists to use theatre as a means of collective self-assessment and a vehicle for exploring the conditions and the potential of their community. How myopic, then, a critical view that evaluates only the interaction of performers and scenic elements on stage during one particular night! How much more revealing a view of that performance in its self-determined context, in its dynamic relationship to the audience and the community. The critic should widen his angle of vision to include the play's effect upon the audience and upon the immediate community. That, of course, would play havoc with the prevailing practice of quick (and often uncomplimentary) reviews which must meet the deadline of the next day. But if the critic "lived-in"—that is, attended a rehearsal or two, "hung out" at the theatre for a few days, moved about in the local neighborhood— a better sense of that production's meaning and achievement within its own context might be forthcoming.

It is clear that audience/community is an essential element in Black theatre. Therefore it too should play a role in the evalua-

[7]Addison Gayle, Jr., ed., *The Black Aesthetic* (New York: Anchor Books, 1971), Introduction, xxii.

tion of the work. Certainly a theatre which conceives itself as a socializing force must be judged, in part, by the size and responsiveness of its audience. As theatre scholar J. L. Styan states, " 'The play' is what an audience perceives. . . . Not only is the printed text merely the score . . . for the actual experience of the play, but the performance itself is not the experience either. It is rather the occasion for stimulus and reaction, in which the meaning and value of the experience reside finally in what an audience takes away."[8]

The formal critical mode, as presently constituted, does not take the audience into account; in fact the critic frequently takes a condescending view of the spectators. For example, Drummond's statement (quoted earlier) about the encounter group atmosphere of the production on Angela Davis does not go far enough. While he records the audience's apparent identification with the events onstage, he fails to ask perhaps the most important questions. Why does the audience make this leap of imagination? Why am I (Drummond) separated from this communal experience?

In the absence of sensitive, useful criticism, theatre artists must generate their own. Some directors, such as Gilbert Moses, invite an interested colleague into rehearsals to observe and critique during the entire process of preparation, performance, and aftermath of the production. Theatre groups, such as Kuumba Players in Chicago, attempt to measure the effect of the play by having discussions with the audience after each performance. Here player and audience communicate directly about the value of the play, the choices of the director, the skill of the performers and many other points which the single reviewer may ignore. Such alternatives are becoming traditions in theatre groups, as they devise their own methods for getting useful and appropriate critical response.

In a theatre which places such emphasis upon mass appeal, it is legitimate to ask whether the critic, the single individual who reviews a production, has a place indeed. If so, what role should this person play? The sensitive and informed critic is very important to Black theatre. He can be a third eye (the first two being

[8]J. L. Styan, "Sight and Space: The Perception of Shakespeare on Stage and Screen," *Educational Theatre Journal,* 29 (1), March 1977, p. 18.

the director's), if he understands the intent of the production, knows its historical development, assesses the skills of the company, and judges the extent to which they achieve their goals. If the stage is to be used as metaphor—the individual as actor, character and human being—then the critic can also write about the theatrical process, that drama which unfolds as the play is prepared. Those who have worked in theatre know that the performance itself is but a small fraction of the miracle represented on stage. The experience of watching a play is frequently enriched by the knowledge one has of the actors, technicians, and the obstacles they have overcome in mounting the show.

The critic, however, is also audience. Given the participatory nature of Black audiences, the critic should lend himself to the production, allowing self to be caught up in the emotional sweep of the event. In a sense, the critic is both ecstatic and intellectual, a participant who can reflect upon the theatre experience with sensitivity and then analyze his personal reaction, as well as that of the audience, to the production. The excitement, thoughts and images (or their opposites) generated by a play should be placed in an ethical perspective so that the viewer may understand more fully his own part. Just as the critic speaks to the performer and director, so he speaks to the audience, expanding the creative moment and interpreting it so that the viewer/reader exclaims, "Yes, that is what I felt. You have given voice to my emotions." Such an analysis presumes the extended influence of the newspaper critic and assumes that the reviewer will represent the reactions of most spectators in recreating as fully as possible the evening's experience. His words should act as a guide, not an ultimatum, for those who were not present. Not only is the critic a creative link between audience and performer, articulating for both, he also provides a permanent record of these elusive but significant moments for present and future generations.

The battle between critics and theatre artists is unnecessary and wasteful. Rigorous assessment is crucial to the artists' development. But Black theatre does not need the condescending, calloused, flippant reviews of uninformed critics. Both performers and audiences need the live-in critic, the observer/participant, as well as direct dialogue with each other. The critic, be it single reviewer or audience, must in turn respect the artist and under-

# Black Critics on Black Theatre
# in America

## by Abiodun Jeyifous

One of the highest priority items among those of us who
are concerned with the history, theory, and criticism of
Afro-American theatre is a redefinition of Afro-American
theatre within the framework of Afro-American culture.
We must not continue to accept a Euro-American concept
of what constitutes a good play or a bad play, how an audience ought to behave, and so on. If we do, we will never
even begin to discover the vast and beautiful and exciting
history of our own theatre.

CARLTON W. MOLETTE, 1970

No one man or single institution can personalize the course
of history, but it seems that in periods of extreme radical awareness and revolutionary confrontation some individuals may seem
to embody the complex forces of historical becoming. Thus,
every critic and enthusiast of contemporary black theatre, even
observers calculatedly cool to its stated goals and aspirations, all
agree on one point: the central role of Imamu Amiri Baraka and
the two theatre groups he founded, the Black Arts Repertory
School and Theatre in Harlem and, later, the Spirit House of
Newark. Larry Neal and Woodie King, Jr., in extensive articles,
and Ed Bullins, in several interviews, have all attempted to re-
construct the factual details and the general outline of what happened in black theatre in that turbulent later half of the sixties.

Extracted from "Black Critics on Black Theatre in America" by Abiodun
Jeyifous. From *The Drama Review*, Vol. 18, No. 3 (T-63, September 1974), pp.
34-45. Reprinted by permission of the author.

It seems that within a general context of an intense radicalization and politicalization of the arts in the country there emerged a distinct movement toward black cultural and political nationalism. Baraka dominated the cultural aspect and, in his own peculiar style, emphasized its political nature.

In 1968 the first *Drama Review* issue on black theatre was published and promptly became the unofficial collective manifesto of the movement, "the black revolutionary theatre," as it was then called. *Black Theatre* magazine, edited by Ed Bullins, also emerged in 1968 as a very vigorous, strongly partisan magazine of the movement, setting the tone of discussion within the movement, the direction and the "correct" line of ideology. The first anthology of the movement had appeared in 1967, titled *Black Fire* and edited by Baraka and Neal. It contained a section on plays, some by young black playwrights who could never have been published in any other kind of anthology, so stark, so overt, so visceral, and so scornful was the nature of their attack on white America and specific targets within the black community. The second anthology, *New Plays from the Black Theatre,* edited by Bullins, appeared in 1969 and, with notable exceptions, featured much the same kind of material. The sole reason for the publication of these plays, their *raison d'être,* was that they appealed spontaneously to the masses of black people before whom they were presented. This became, in the manifestoes and self-evaluative articles written by members and partisans of the movement, the overriding criterion, the source of other criteria by which the revolutionary black theatre was to be judged. Thus, *consciousness* replaced *sensibility* as the basic parameter of black theatre criticism. Later, with the firm establishment of major black theatre groups, their production of more exploratory and experimental material, much critical debate, and many symposia, the terms of the new cohesive critical criteria were broadened, refined, and deepened, often through intensely bitter and fractious quarrels and debates.

It is necessary for a proper appreciation of the present black critical trend to emphasize three aspects of the black revolutionary theatre movement that were so totally unprecedented in previous black theatre in this country that they have dominated critical discussion and no doubt will continue to dominate it for a long time to come. First, there was the radical and complete rejection of the commercial theatre, particularly its values but also its presumed esthetic premises. Second, there was the equally radical insistence that black theatre would be legitimized by the black community *only,* legitimized by specific reference to its specific history, its culture and over-all situation in America—all often emphasized in their uniqueness *and* radical opposition to white American culture and "mainstream" traditions. The third aspect is one whose importance has not been stressed enough. This is the essential unity, in the initial phase of the movement, of the critical and creative functions in the new black theatre and the continuing influence in criticism of playwrights, directors, and producers.

This third point needs careful re-stating. Baraka, Bullins, Ronald Miller, Tom Dent, John O'Neal, Robert Macbeth, Barbara Ann Teer, and others were not only lawgivers unto themselves, but they also forced others to reckon with them in terms *they* proposed, in terms they generated in their art and work. They were able to do this because they were genuine creators and innovators. As they wrote manifestoes and issued critical broadsides, they *built* functioning and disciplined groups, wrote plays, prodigiously created improvised enactments ("rituals"), and experimented ceaselessly with new forms, new ideas. Significantly, their best interpreters (such as Larry Neal and Clayton Riley) were partisans intimately connected with them by a commonality of aspirations and ideological persuasion, thereby proving, in the face of the rigorously fragmented, specialized separation of critical and creative tasks in the American theatre, that both functions are, in the best of conditions, ultimately inseparable.

The inculcation of "community" and "consciousness" as basic parameters of black theatre criticism led to the establishment of critical canons by which black critics analyzed the theatre. In a 1969 symposium, Baraka stated what these canons are:

> I would like to...say that my conception of art, black art, is that it has to be collective, it has to be functional, it has to be committed and that actually, if it's not stemming from conscious nationalism, then at this time it's invalid. When I say collective, that it comes from the collective experience of black people, when I say committed, it has to be committed to change, revolutionary change. When I say functional, it has to have a function to the lives of black people.

Collective, committed, functional. There is no denying that these standards soon became a rigidified system because of easy application by many of the younger black critics in the pages of such magazines as *Black Theatre* and *Negro Digest (Black World,* as it was renamed). As Larry Neal says, "there's nothing as distasteful as a formalized esthetic." However, there is no question about the depth and subtlety of the understanding of these canons by black theatre artists like Baraka himself or Barbara Ann Teer or its careful elaboration by critics like Riley and Neal. In effect, these criteria became rooted in cultural patterns of the black community. This might be demonstrated by showing the attachment of each criterion to a cultural norm. "Functionality," for instance, became tied to the attitude of black people toward their traditional performance modes, and there was the demand that a performance, or an expressive display or form be efficacious socially, ritually, or religiously, as the case may be. But what is more important is an account of the elaboration of unique perceptual and expressive modes within black culture and how these should serve as the theoretical props of a truly black theatre.

Consider the following account by Langston Hughes of the presentation of Eugene O'Neill's *The Emperor Jones* in a Harlem theatre house of the twenties and thirties:

> The audience didn't know what to make of *The Emperor Jones* on a stage where "Shake That Thing" was formerly the rage. And when the Emperor started running naked through the forest, hearing the Little Frightened Fears, naturally they howled with laughter.
>
> "Them ain't no ghosts, fool!," the spectators cried from the orchestra,
> "Why don't you come on out o' that jungle back to Harlem where you belong?"
>
> In the manner of Stokowski hearing a cough at the Academy of Music, Jules Bledsoe stopped dead in his tracks, advanced to the footlights, and proceeded to lecture his audience on manners in the theatre. But the audience wanted none of *The Emperor Jones.* And their manners had been all right at all the other shows.... So when Brutus continued his flight, the audience again howled with laughter. And that was the end of *The Emperor Jones* on 135th Street.

Within conventional (Western) criticism this response would be written off as a reflection of the axiom that art or drama can only happen at a certain level (social class) of appreciation. But to the black theatre artists and critics this was indicative of their precise contention that art and theatre are merely agglomerations of culturally matrixed conventions and usages. It is clear that the appreciative or responsive capacity of the audience is not vulgar and defective but that the conventions of theatrical illusionism and textual dramaturgy have been culturally displaced and hence are "defective." Only this awareness can explain the following "heresy" from Larry Neal:

Open up, black writers. Open up. Blow. Yeah, blow those white dreams and demons away. Kill the beast of a fetid literary tradition. Blow them away. Open up. Link up with the struggle. Confront yourselves. Do your thing whenever and wherever you can. Talk to each other. Your own magazines and journals. Your own films and playhouses. Your own critique. White writers can teach you very little. Perhaps some precise kind of technique. But Stevie Wonder's technique is finally hipper than T.S. Eliot's. Talk to each other. No alienation in white liberal zones. Embrace black people; experiment with black styles. What, for example, is the meaning of the bugaloo? I mean it. James Brown is the best poet we got baby.

The reference to James Brown is a very precise metaphor for the *kind* of black theatre being called and willed into existence here— James Brown and the incomparable poise of the pantomimic postures, the alternation of elegant freezes and flawlessly smooth gliding motions which accompany his music and song, themselves rooted in the traditional styles and idiom.

Within the new black critical nomenclature, there are definitive positions and prescriptions: the oral nature of communicative patterns in the black community and the special relationship to the word (as a fusion of indexical image and pure sound); the central place of song, dance, and music in all black performance modes, and in particular the centrality of music as a communicative mode where there is always reciprocity of relations between language/speech and music (the voice as a register of emotions and musical instrumentation as the extension of the voice and consequently that register); native forms of humor, satire, parody, comedy, and coded grapevine; the existence of a mythic lore, traditional and contemporary; and religious and secular rituals of death, play, conflict, sexuality. Realism and "rituals" dominate contemporary black theatre. As used by black artists both stylistic forms are under attack by both white and black critics. White critics see realism in black theatre as a throwback to an outmoded, tired Western style. Some black critics see realism as a deadened, a reactionary style since it tends to be too faithful a mirror of the present desperation and harassed condition of existence in the black urban ghettos. ("After pimps, pushers, whores, venal preachers, hustlers, dope fiends, the general alienated existence, what next?" goes the question.) A lot of white and black critics simply regard the "rituals" in bemused wonderment.

Since black playwrights, such as Ed Bullins, who use realism, and some black critics speak of their usage of that style as a kind of black neo-realism predicated on life-styles, mannerisms, and "gests" within the black community, it would seem that special canons of appreciation are demanded for the two dominant forms in black theatre. This has led to the proposition that the black experience, or a deep appreciation and awareness of it, is an indispensable factor in this regard. The following casual remarks are from Baraka at a black theatre forum called together by Woodie King, Jr., at the Gate Theatre, Lower East Side, New York in 1969:

> Like a critic is valuable if he has the same value system as the writer. If we are like one people and we have the same values, then what he says is valuable to me, because its going to be in tune with what I think anyway and he can point out things that I don't do. You see. But if he has a totally different value system, if he's representing Euro-American, Judeo-Christian, you know—decadism— (laughter).
>
> Then he speaks of something I've done or Ed's [Bullins] done, it's a totally different thing. It don't relate. Like the white boy says about a play like *Jello.* "This is a terrible play and it's a racist play, and it's doing this and that and it's horrible." Then you take it out on the street and people laugh at it, you know, black people think it's funny because it's a different value system. A lot of the people who own theatres have different value systems, even though they might, you know, be colored. ...

Of realism, Paul Carter Harrison thinks that

> social realism is at the heart of the problem: it deters the fullest ex-
> cavation of hidden meanings by locking images into fixed relation-
> ships with the surfaces of social life. The mode becomes static. Our
> senses are guided toward reinforcing the obvious; all motivations
> are limited to the obvious context.

But he sees a way out, through a relentless penetration of the crust
of fixed social experience to potentialities of the spirit:

> We must go with the negative to its corruptive terminal point of
> realization, its scorned bestiality, its violent destruction through the
> re-living of its horrible aspects, its total devouring of the nerve end-
> ings until our souls are shipwrecked....

Of "rituals," Larry Neal uses a practical and subtly effective
criterion of judgment:

> Barbara Ann Teer of the National Black Theatre, for example,
> moved away from the crafted play and toward a ritualist theatre.
> Teer's pieces are big, with many performers, and she uses her work
> in a functional manner—at the Congress of African People last
> year, she opened up one of the sessions by moving her whole
> brightly costumed troupe into a huge auditorium, carrying red,
> black, and green flags, singing, chanting, dancing down the aisles.
> Her texts for the rituals are unimportant and corny, but her com-
> pany's energy is extraordinary—proved by the fact that they played
> the Apollo Theatre, successfully.
>   You never could put one of Robert Macbeth's New Lafayette
> rituals in the Apollo. The New Lafayette rituals are, for me (and
> such reactions are very personal) failures, failures of energy. Their
> modality is oriental, characterized by silence and darkness....
> They tend to be slow, plodding, studious, and done with a very
> solemn air. Pieces open in a darkened theatre, perhaps to symbolize
> a plunge into the inner self. An off-stage voice lays down the text,
> which is too long, and too mysterious. The only reason to stress all
> this is that when ideology is removed from the rhythms and vigor
> of the people on whom it is based, it becomes self-defeating and
> cannot be made into meaningful images and gestures. *(Perfor-
> mance*, April 1972)

Larry Neal wrote these words in 1972, by which time there was
beginning to be very audible in black theatre criticism a mel-

lowed tone and a detached wariness about the work of black theatre artists, an eventuality that contrasted with the earlier revolutionary fervor and partisan, enthusiastic solidarity with black theatre artists. Much of present black critical writing is understandably concerned with revaluations, while occasional reviews by a Clayton Riley or a Peter Bailey relate the specific work to the critic's vision of what would, at this time, be a true black theatre.

In the last ten years since Baraka's *Dutchman* was written and produced, not only have there been more producing black groups formed, more plays have been written (literally in the hundreds) than in the previous 130 years since the African Grove Company of New York started the first black theatre company in the country in the 1820's. The best black American playwrights are not only among the best in the country but among the best writing anywhere (where "best" means the chance meeting of talent, mature vision, and a vigorous theatre to work in). It is difficult to recall the extraordinary nature of this phenomenon in recorded theatre history.

Against the established achievements of black theatre, however, there also has been considerable regression in the past couple of years. This development has been caused, no doubt, by the great problems black theatre artists have encountered in their decision to confront their historical mission to repossess their fragmented selves, which have been trailing after the American theatre's distortion of the black image. The avowed aim of black theatre is "to raise the consciousness" of black people to an awareness of who they are. Many black theatre artists have come to an appreciation—some by instinctive, visceral experience, many by conscious, deliberate analysis—of the immense difficulties of "raising consciousness" in a social order whose inner logic *needs* human ghettos of the order of South Africa's *Bantustans.* I think the deluge of the contemporary "black" movies, the sight of rivers of black people flocking to the Broadway district to see updated versions of stereotypes of black people long hallowed in the American theatre and film, to see images of death, bestiality, mindlessness, this more than anything else, more than the chronic financial troubles, has precipitated that recognition by black theatre artists. In many cases, despite some notable exceptions (Baraka, John O'Neal, Barbara Ann Teer) who have held on to their revolutionary commitment to change the existing realities, the weight of this recognition has engendered a whole variety of responses, all tending to be reactionary. This is probably the reason why Baraka issued a recent scathing critique of some companies and artists that insiders within the black theatre community could not but recognize.

Also a great many of the theatre companies that were once Black are still "Black" but hardly revolutionary. They often have become fixed and stylized, and individualistic elitist celebrant cults for gigantic egos, to boot.

In these conditions, the function of the black critic becomes particularly onerous and vaguely reminiscent of the kind of theatre criticism encountered in Harold Cruse's monumental critique of black middle-class artists and intellectuals, *The Crisis of the Negro Intellectual*, where, having offered penetrating and often devastating criticism of the historical situation, problems, and work of many established black theatre artists, Cruse *had* to offer nostrums for specified problems but comes a cropper on this point. I think the obvious moral is that some problems will be solved, in the words of Fanon, not on the level of theory but in the field of revolutionary practice. This makes understandable the critical hesitation noticeable among some sensitive black critics at this period, as implied in these remarks by Clayton Riley at a recent panel discussion on black theatre criticism:

I don't think there's a black theatre. ... There isn't a black theatre that anybody can define or anybody can locate really, on a regular, on a consistent basis. ... Black theatre is and has been for a number of years a rather hit or miss thing.

What I'd like to talk about is why I think this is true. The reason there isn't a black theatre, and understand one thing, that there isn't a consistently present one, it's simply because Americans aren't interested in what black people do in America. The only people who I think at this point, on a general basis, are interested are black people. The unfortunate thing about that situation is that black people at this point in time just don't have the money to support the theatre; there are too many other things that have to take a priority. I don't know whether that ought to be the case or not. But it is.

# Two Views by White Critics:
# (1) Must I Side with Blacks or Whites?

*by Eric Bentley*

I can't think of any theater I would rather sit down in than the New Lafayette at Seventh Avenue and 137th Street, just around the corner from Mother Zion Church. It is an auditorium that combines the best of both worlds—the hospitable informality of Off Off Broadway buildings and the comfortable formality of conventional theaters with seats fixed to the floor and arranged in neat rows. It's nice also because they don't have the house lights on full before the show. "A dim religious light" burns, as does incense which, however, has an odor agreeably unsuggestive of either the Pope or the Maharishi: a hedonistic, irreligious incense.

It's also a good place to see a show. There are three banks of seats, two of them raised high, stadium-fashion. The audience sits on three sides of the spectacle, which is on the floor, not on a stage. For the show I saw there, "The Psychic Pretenders," this floor was covered with carpets of different colors, and these colors became different again and again in the constant play of a color wheel. A charming effect and, in the course of the evening. I found it to be typical of the whole show in its subtle combination of turbulence and regularity, energy and repose.

The subtitle is "Pageant of the Black Passion in Three Motions." The "motions" are through three gates, the gate of the searchers, the gate of love, and the gate of intuitive knowledge. In other words, the whole thing is a quest, a story of trial-by-ordeal, of education and growing-up, of a type familiar to many of us

"Must I Side with Blacks or Whites?" by Eric Bentley. From the *New York Times,* January 23, 1972. © 1966/72 by The New York Times Company. Reprinted by permission.

from Bunyan's "Pilgrim's Progress" and Mozart's "The Magic Flute."

The special twist here is that the pilgrim is black. This brings about an inversion of the familiar color scheme. Whereas in "The Magic Flute," the villain is a queen of blackest night, and the black man in the same opera, Monostatos, is a blend of barbarian and devil, while both the young hero and his ancient mentor are pillars of white civilization, in "The Psychic Pretenders" the mentor is a black mother-figure, while the pilgrim is a black youth whose problem is that he wears a white mask and white pants. That is, he is pretending to be white, he has gone over to the enemy. He will be making headway in the degree that he is reclaimed by blackness. Regress to the black maternal womb will be this pilgrim's progress—this prodigal's return, not to Heavenly Father, but to Earthly Mother.

"The Psychic Pretenders" is not an opera but neither is it what most people would consider a straight play. On a high platform at the back of the floor-space are several musicians who play almost uninterruptedly from beginning to end. A good score, redolent of Africa and New Orleans, mostly a drum used with delicacy. Even the trombone is delicate in this combo, not the same instrument you've heard in a brass band. There is spoken dialogue, but not much, and it is rather less distinguished, I thought, than the non-verbal elements. You watch the actors a great deal more intently than you listen to them. Call it a dance drama: there is plenty of outright dance, all movements are large and ceremonious. It is a spectacle that is choreographed throughout.

It is a work of art but what kind of art, exactly? And what is art, anyway? I ask this last question advisedly because it is categorically answered in the program, an amazing fact when you consider that this program does not even give the name of the author or the composer, nor tell which actor plays which role, nor yet explain the quite obscure title of the show. "The raising of consciousness," says this otherwise reticent document, "...is the purpose of art." Having always wondered what the purpose of art was myself, I cannot but admire such glorious self-confidence. In the afterglow of reading this, I'll even overlook, for the moment, all the art that has *not* been dedicated to raising of consciousness (at least in the sense here intended).

In any case I am among those who, today, welcome all art that does make a respectable stab at raising consciousness, and obviously this is the task to which all black literature, all black art, addresses itself today.

A Community Art Institution takes on responsibility for the creation and presentation of images which are vivid enough to activate the minds of the community audience to considerations of their everyday existence from points of view consistent with that community's place in history and its efforts toward the future.

That's our program again. To activate people's minds. Get them to see what's happening to them. By means of images. So that what is *called* a community—Harlem, in this case—might *become* a community. So that a bunch of paupers and semi-slaves might become a family of fully human beings. Through solidarity to power and fulfillment. It's a beautiful conception.

What success black theater is having in raising consciousness I am not equipped to say, and in the nature of things it is hard to measure. What a non-black observer can observe is the very considerable variety of approaches among black theater people, and "The Psychic Pretenders" strikes me as far more successful than the naturalistic efforts I've seen, such as the current "Black Terror" at the Public Theater, written, as it happens, by one of the Playwrights in Residence at the New Lafayette, Richard Wesley.

"The Black Terror" comes across as a conventional—in that sense, white—play which, by the appropriate conventional standards simply does not make the grade. Even if it were a better piece of writing and of playmaking—even *more* so then—one would have to ask what messages actually come through, and not just what messages the playwright may have intended to send. At the Public Theater, this "black" work simply confirms for the largely white audience what White America has brought them up to believe about Terrorism in general and Terrorism by "Nigras" in particular, namely that all terrorists are nuts and black terrorists are savages into the bargain. Any comparisons between this play and "The Battle of Algiers," or even with "La Chinoise," are entirely unearned. Its effect, as opposed to its intention, is reactionary and racist.

If Richard Wesley ends up making use of the white man's stereotype of the Black (the native, the savage, the cannibal, the Hottentot), what shall we say of equally "farout" cartoon images of the villainous White Man? The strongest piece of theater I have seen in the past couple of years is "Slave Ship" by LeRoi Jones, as produced in 1969 at the Chelsea Theater Center. Where Wesley merely falls backwards into racism, Jones leaps delightedly into it, face-forwards. What is the white theatergoer to do? Stay away from Jones' plays? Play at being Black? That surely is an effort at identification with the victim which soon becomes ludicrous. Enjoy being put down by such a fanatic down-putter? That surely is an exercise in white masochism that only black sadists can contemplate with satisfaction. White middle class liberals can be counted on for a goodly amount of breast beating, it is true, but not for this much. As for myself, though I'm as guilt-ridden as the next man, I didn't really feel guiltier for seeing Jones' play, for, rightly or wrongly, I just didn't identify myself with the Whites in it. How could one? They were monsters.

Then I identified myself—sentimentally—with the Blacks? Not that, either. Not that *exactly*. Feeling detached from both groups, I found myself, quite instinctively, taking the play as an image of all such struggles. Finally, I did identify myself with the Blacks but for me they weren't necessarily black. They were yellow, and from Vietnam. They were red, and from Manhattan. They were white-skinned and black with coal-dust like the miners of Lancashire, England, where I come from.

As a Socialist, I read LeRoi Jones' play as a series of extremely vivid images of capitalist exploitations, and this is not something I thought of later, it is only my later formulation of what I was actually feeling during the performance. So, as a Socialist, I got my consciousness raised by a writer who (I must assume) wants me liquidated as a carrier of the white plague; and whom I disapprove of as a racist.

A few years ago, most white people would have said that anti-White literature was, by definition, racist. It is not necessarily so. In "The Psychic Pretenders," two Blacks produce a little white baby doll with the stars and stripes painted on it. They light matches, as if to burn it. Symbolically speaking, it *is* burnt. Such an incident is typical of "The Psychic Pretenders" but, as I see things, did not have the force of racism because, in this work, though certainly white culture is seen as the enemy, the extermination of white men is not seen as the remedy. Rather, the drawing apart of black men *from* the white culture.

Here's an analogy. In Vietnam, The American is the enemy, and is fair game for the satirist as well as for the anti-aircraft gunner. This is not to say that the Vietnamese represent any threat to the American people, let alone that they encourage racist doctrines that would include themselves "in" and most of us "out."

When I call "The Psychic Pretenders" more successful than "The Black Terror," I am ignoring economics: "The Black Terror" may well be earning more money. Can black theaters ignore economics? Hardly: the dependence of many of them on white foundations is notorious. The issues are complex, but come down to Lenin's who/whom? Are the foundations buying off the revolutionaries, or are the revolutionaries taking advantage of the foundations?

Again, some people see a theater in the ghetto as principally a way of bringing culture to the uneducated. This process carries the reactionary implication of opium for the people. Should black theaters refuse money from white foundations? Or would this be a display of unrealistic idealism, futile pride? Why doesn't the ghetto itself support ghetto theaters? Because they are too radical? Because they are too arty, and the ghetto prefers Channel 2?

The problems are those of the theater of commitment generally. There are probably no pure solutions or, if there are, they may not be better than some of the impure ones. Or purer. The contradictions will be there, willy nilly. If anything is certain, it is that results will be achieved, not by living in dread of the contradictions or contemptuously rejecting them, but by taking for granted that they are going to be there. Working "with" them, yes, but working against them—working through them.

# Two Views by White Critics:
# (2) Enroute to the Future

*by Stanley Kauffmann*

In an age of multiple revolutions, the theater is having at least one of its own. More and more frequently, Negro actors are playing white roles.

The implications are profound. If the movement continues (and there is reason to think it will grow) the result will be an even more momentous revolution in the audience. Theater managers and directors are engaging Negroes for a variety of motives: enlightened judgment, cynical exploitation of topicality, artistically misguided liberalism. Whatever the motives, their actions at present put them considerably in advance of much of the public; and since, in the realm of ideas, the theater usually lags about one full generation behind the public, this is extraordinary news.

I am not talking about the Hollywood complaints that the racial proportions of our population are inadequately reflected in the writing of scripts. Nor do I mean the creation of roles for Negroes that, a few years ago, would automatically have been written for whites—such as TV private eyes. I mean roles, usually in the standard repertory, that were written for white actors—*characters* who are white—and are now being played by Negroes in mixed casts.

In opera the postwar years have brought us a number of Negro singers in white roles, such as Camilla Williams, Mattiwilda Dobbs and, most notably, Leontyne Price. But opera lives by its own scale of realism. If we can accept a corseted old buttertub as a winsome young maiden just because she has a glorious voice, it is a relatively slight adjustment to accept a Negro in a white role for the same reason.

It is not brand new practice in the theater. The common starting point for discussion is Ira Aldridge, the Negro actor who was born in Maryland in 1804 and who won fame in numerous heroic roles, including Othello, but he did virtually all his acting abroad. Othello has been the obvious gate for many Negro actors into the white theater; still when Paul Robeson played it here in 1943, there was endless immaterial debate as to whether "Moor" means "Negro." The practice of mixed casting remained so unsteady that when Canada Lee played in Webster's "Duchess of Malfi" with Elizabeth Bergner in 1946, he "whited up" for his part.

The first Negro actor I can remember seeing in a white role in a mixed cast was Jack Carter, who played Mephistopheles in Marlowe's "Dr. Faustus" when Orson Welles directed it for the Federal Theater in 1937. The practice has not grown until the last few years. Now Negroes are (or recently have been) playing white roles at the Tyrone Guthrie Theater in Minneapolis, the Lincoln Center Repertory Theater, the Ypsilanti Greek Theater, the New York Shakespeare Festival, the Stratford (Conn.) Shakespeare Festival, the Berkshire Theater Festival and elsewhere.

In nonrealistic plays, the process is almost as easily accommodated as in opera. If nobody in Vienna recognizes the Duke in "Measure for Measure" merely because he puts on different dress, why should we strain at the fact that some of the Viennese are Negroes?

But when we get to realistic drama, the process becomes more difficult and the implications are greater. In the Guthrie Theater production of Strindberg's "Dance of Death," all the actors are white except the young man who plays the son of the principal couple. The veristic texture of the play makes his color a small shock. It would be stupid to pretend otherwise. But it is exactly that shock that has to be faced at present so that it can subside into custom. I suppose that, in Restoration England, oldtimers who could remember the theater before Cromwell were shocked at seeing women on the stage.

What is the alternative to mixed casting? Eleven percent of this country's population is Negro, and we need no census to tell us how theatrically talented many Negroes are. Must Negro actors be confined to plays about Negroes or to Negro characters in otherwise white plays? That has been the prevailing practice, and it is insufficient on grounds of common justice and healthy art. It cuts off Negro actors from the world's heritage of great drama, unless they go away and do plays (as they used to do, at the Lafayette Theater in Harlem) where they won't bother the white folks. It cuts off Negro actors from the flow of new plays and the building of new theaters. It cuts off the public from invigorating talents. Are we to maintain a segregation in the theater that we are trying to eliminate in every other aspect of our life?

I do not argue that statistical rules should prevail, that 11 per cent of all casts should be Negro. Artistic standards should apply — more strenuously, I would hope, than they have always applied in the past, But that is precisely the point. *Only* artistic standards should apply, not those of color or of any other kind.

Obviously there will always be some exceptions. For example, if a plot depends on differences between Negroes and whites, then that fact would naturally control the casting. But in the vast majority of plays, where color is of no consequence to the plot, it ought to be of no consequence to the casting.

I know that I have put the matter simply, that there are shades and complexities. Two years ago, when Diana Sands played in "The Owl and the Pussycat," I thought that the coherence of that particular play would have benefited by a few references to her color. In the Minneapolis production of Strindberg, a hint of civil-rights fervor touches the presence of the young Negro as the white couple's son, because he is only a modestly acceptable actor and we cannot help suspecting an ulterior motive in this casting. On the other hand, in a film called "Duel at Diablo," where a lot of unlikely things happen to a Negro in the old West, we make all kinds of concessions to the unlikelihood because otherwise we would have missed Sidney Poitier's performance.

So the process has begun and, *with artistic aptness alone as the criterion,* must continue. In the July 15 [1966] issue of the (London) New Statesman, their American correspondent Andrew Kopkind wrote of our present racial agony: "The dream of an integrated national community is about over.... The country has responded to Negroes' demands over the past decade primarily by eliminating the symbols of southern feudalism.... Otherwise, there have been few changes in American institutions." With Mr. Kopkind's bitter impatience I sympathize; but there is one institution that has seen radical changes. The employment of Negro actors in the American theater—as a whole—has been more than "tokenism." It must now grow to be a matter of artistic course.

This will mean—it has already meant—a profound change in the social vision of the audience. I am not talking about some muzzy utopia in which no one notices the color of anyone else's skin. (Imagine ignoring Diahann Carroll's color!) I mean that in a theater in which Jews play Gentiles and Gentiles play Jews, in which Americans play foreigners and vice versa—in short, where power of conviction is the crux—the subordination of the facts of life to the facts of art should also apply to color.

All art lives by convention, which means factual unreality for the sake of larger truth. Now theatrical convention is being extended: so that the actor who is best for a role—in ability, temperament and physique—can be engaged, regardless of color. Skin tone soon becomes irrelevant in performance.

And this new theatrical circumstance can help the general change in social values, even in neural responses, that—flatly and absolutely—must occur in the future, if there is to be a future.

It is necessary, this change of view. It is beautiful. Our theater —so often bedraggled, stale and false—has, in this aspect at least, begun to be inspiriting and true. Civilized men and women can hope that the procedure will spread; for the American theater, in the third quarter of this century, there is no civilized alternative.

# Black Theater:
# The Search Goes On

*by Lindsay Patterson*

I remember quite well the first Broadway musical I ever saw. It was a touring company of *Porgy and Bess* with Leontyne Price and William Warfield. I didn't like it much, probably because I had just recently learned to say "am not" for "ain't" and to pronounce consonants at the end of words, and I was furious at having to sit in a segregated balcony. So, it was with great satisfaction that I witnessed *Porgy and Bess* (along with Amos and Andy and Stepin Fetchit) fall into disgrace during the sixties. But I've learned the hard way that nothing is absolute—what is in disfavor today will eventually be resurrected and justified tomorrow.

That's why it is not surprising that the Metropolitan Opera will present *Porgy and Bess* during the bicentennial year as its token black offering. What is surprising, though, is that the black classical musical *establishment* has not demanded that a Black playwright and a Black musician be commissioned to create a work for the occasion. Leontyne Price, offered the part of Bess, declined it (I'm certain) on the grounds of musical integrity which is her personal and artistic right. But the Metropolitan Opera has no excuse for offering any Black artist anything less than an original work, since most of the musical forms spawned in America before and during its short two hundred year old republican history have black antecedents. And too, there is every indication that the black musical theater—which formed the basis for the Broadway musical—is in for a revival.

"Black Theater: The Search Goes On" by Lindsay Patterson. From *Freedomways,* Vol. 14, No. 3 (1974), pp. 242-46. Reprinted by permission of *Freedomways* magazine, published at 799 Broadway, New York City.

J. E. Franklin, author of *Black Girl*, Micki Grant, composer and lyricist for *Don't Bother Me I Can't Cope*, and choreographer Rod Rodgers pooled their talents last summer to produce *The Prodigal Sister*. Other playwrights, choreographers and composers are talking and planning how they, too, can come together and present a total cultural experience. But whether a full-fledged revival of the black musical theater is in the offing (or a continuation of black dramatic theater as experienced in the sixties) will depend upon neighborhood theaters in New York, and, at the moment, their future—with or without the Met's cooperation—seems bleak.

Last year, many of us were profoundly shocked at the closing of the New Lafayette Theatre in Harlem. A theater for which we had high hopes, since it seemed to have everything going for it: a prime location in Harlem, generous grants and the handsomest and most functional interior of any Off-Broadway theater in New York. When I asked Ed Bullins, the New Lafayette's chief resident playwright, why the theater had closed, he said rather tersely that "It's time had come"; but Woodie King, director of the active New Federal Theater, disagrees with that assertion.

"They presented plays not in tune with what the community was about," says King. "It was no different for that community to go to the Lafayette than to a play downtown, and the only writer they used of any interest to the community was Ed Bullins.

"Also, black audiences want realistic plays," asserts King. "They want plays like Bullins' *In New England Winter, Goin' a Buffalo*, and *The Fabulous Miss Marie*. Those plays had no trouble attracting an audience, until they started alienating artists, audience and critics. The audience said, 'I don't need this.' Why should they go through changes to go into a theater. And too, they alienated their funding sources, not by what they said, but by what they presented. And in some cases there were some problems with the artistic level of excellence in comparison with the amount of money they had. If you're getting three or four hundred thousand dollars and you're paying your actors three or four hundred dollars, the technical level has to be commensurate with your artistic level. For an example, at that time, James Earl Jones was a three or four hundred dollar a week actor, but they didn't use people of that quality. They did have some stunning performers, but they were feature players, and feature players could not pull into that theater what was needed."

King's own theater is part of the Henry Street Settlement, which is located on the lower East Side in a neighborhood composed largely of Blacks, Puerto Ricans and Asians. Incomes are low and many of its youthful residents have never strayed much beyond its borders; yet, most of the New Federal Theatre's productions attract capacity crowds, while many other neighborhood theaters have great difficulty in attracting even minimal audiences.

"Low income people in New York," declares King, "cannot deal with the term theater. The word must be destroyed (as far as they are concerned). Having grown up in the city, theater means to them Broadway where the Kennedys and the Javitses go before or after dinner. And the cost of that theater they relate to the word theater no matter where it's located."

To counteract this attitude, King instituted an "opendoor" policy in which audiences are verbally asked to contribute, or given envelopes with the word "contribution" stamped on them. Never is there a suggested contribution, a ploy which many neighborhood theaters use to embarrass patrons into "voluntarily" paying a median admission price. The policy, says King, "has been quite successful."

King asserts that although very few plays can survive or be successful in New York unless they are Black, Puerto Rican, ethnically oriented, or directed toward a specific audience—there are still tremendous pitfalls. For one does not just present an ethnic play; it has to be the right one for your community, and the theater director must realize that within every group there are a wide variety of people and artistic interpretations which can only be properly presented or represented by using a wide variety of writers and directors. These are important facts which King thinks the New Lafayette's management ignored.

"There is no one concept in theater," King advises. "That's why Joseph Papp is very successful. He had the good sense not to try and direct everything. He used anybody who would come in and do it, but under his rules. That's what the New Lafayette needed. I don't try and do everything myself. Running a theater is a matter of selecting people to work with you."

Perhaps, the most fortunate aspect of the New Federal Theatre's operation is that it does not have to depend entirely upon grants or admissions for survival. It could, at a much reduced level, "survive for about ten or fifteen years" on endowment alone. "I couldn't do several plays a year," states King, "but I could do three or four, and I couldn't embellish them or make them as highly professional as we think they are. We would go back in a sense to the community theater tradition."

But what if the theater had no endowment or grants? Could it then survive? "Not by plays alone," says King, "but I could put on something that would make money to stay there." In fact, musical acts are regularly presented at the New Federal Theatre, and draw its largest audiences.

All the principles King has learned in successfully managing the New Federal Theatre, he is certain would work in Harlem. While a theater in that community has to be black, he concedes, it also has to be multi-conceptional. "The ideal theater center there," he asserts, "would be a theater run by Robert Macbeth, Leonard Parker, myself, Dorothy Maynor, Barbara Ann Teer, Ernie McClintock and whoever else. That's the only way it's going to work, because one person does not have the answer. A lot of people think they really know, but this is the age of merging. Everybody's merging. If ITT and ATT can merge, Black people can merge. They have to merge, otherwise, nothing's going to happen. I would merge with anyone to become a stronger unit."

King's idea of merging is an excellent one. A strong, diverse theater unit would assure access to important money sources, reduce administrative and maintenance costs, and probably attract endowment funds. In short, the theater could set its sights on becoming a permanent institution.

But its survival would seem doubtful, since few artistic institutions with consortium managements have yet been able to figure out how to exist without being wrecked by petty in-fighting and political squabbling. Another danger—no less real—would be that the theater unit would consider itself so secure and powerful that it would engage in a fruitless vendetta against critics (as happened for a time with the New Lafayette).

Critics are vital to any art form, for they instruct, chastise, spot trends and sometimes suggest—right or wrongly—what might best suit an individual artist's talents. They are especially needed for the Black community, because much of what is happening there artistically, not only goes unreported, but unevaluated. What does get evaluated is often more an emotional than accurate assessment, and this has been tragic for black theater, both on and off Broadway.

Of the several dozen black plays that have been staged in New York during the last decade and a half, only a handful come anywhere near being absolute entities. That is, the playwright has constructed a world so complete that we do not have to grope outside of the play to supply it with ideas not inherent in the work itself. Characterization, plot and any ideas the author wishes to bombard us with stand up and flow to a full, logical and satisfactory conclusion, as *A Raisin in the Sun, Ceremonies in Dark Old Men, Dutchman* and *No Place to Be Somebody,* do.

There are scores of other black plays which just miss being complete entities, and which, if good black critical hands had been consistently at work, probably would never have been staged before they reached a minimal state of completeness. As it is, Black critics (because they are not employed full time as critics) pay more attention to the reaction of the audiences than to the play, and white critics lower their standards when reviewing black works.

Plays have always reflected the social and political struggles in society; and black plays, certainly, have been no exception. But in the last decade and a half, enough black plays emerged so that the playwrights began to look beyond social and political concerns to artistic concepts and movements. None, however, got very far off the ground. The *black aesthetic* concept fizzled from lack of adequate definition, and *ritual theater* seemingly still remains a concept voiced by playwrights who don't understand theater craft very well. But no artistic movement, concept or trend will develop sufficiently if there aren't persons around who persistently observe and interpret them.

During the past year, I asked many theater artists if they thought black theater was alive and well. Everyone agreed it was very much alive, for there is certainly enough evidence around to support the fact that if not exactly well, it is still actively gasping for breath and direction. It is, in spite of its many infirmities, becoming mature. Younger playwrights are grudgingly learning that theater is a craft, and regardless of whether it's an abhorred

Western form or not, if you're going to use the Western stage to exhibit blackness or anything else, there are certain rules, regulations and limitations which you can't ignore if you want to make a lucid and effective point. Mass Black audiences, like mass audiences anywhere, want, especially to be entertained.

If black theater is to continue to mature or be infused with new ideas, new forms and new points of view, it must find a way to sustain neighborhood theaters.

# Chronology of Important Events

1821    The African Company organized in New York City by Mr. Brown, company manager, with James Hewlett as leading actor.

1823    *King Shotoway* by Mr. Brown; first known play written by an Afro-American produced by the African Company.

1825    Ira Aldridge arrives in London to begin professional acting career; he performs for forty-two years throughout Europe, Russia, and the British Isles.

1843    Dan Emmett with his Virginia Minstrels, a White quartet, officially introduces Negro minstrelsy on the American stage.

1852    *Uncle Tom's Cabin,* adapted for the stage from Harriet Beecher Stowe's famed novel, begins an unprecedented run of eighty years; a version of the play is performed somewhere in the United States regularly until 1932.

1858    *The Escape, or A Leap for Freedom* by ex-slave William Wells Brown published.

1865    Georgia Minstrels, first Black minstrel troupe, organized by Charles Hicks.

1871    Fisk Jubilee Singers on tour of America and Europe with Negro spirituals.

1870s-  B. J. Ford (1878) and J. A. Arneaux leading Black Shake-
1890    spearean actors of the period; they perform in their own Black companies such as the Astor Place Coloured Tragedy Company; Arneaux publishes an edited version of *Richard III* in 1886.

1891    Sam Jack's *The Creole Show* opens in Boston, admitting Black women performers in musical revue.

1896    Worth's Museum All-Star Stock Company founded in New York City by Bob Cole, who begins the first training school for Black performers.

1898    Bob Cole and Billy Johnson team up to produce "musical operettas," their first show being *A Trip to Coontown.*

1900    Bert Williams and George Walker produce their first musical show on Broadway, *The Sons of Ham;* in 1903, their production of *In Dahomey* is taken to London, where it plays a command performance for royalty; their successful partnership ends with Walker's premature death in 1911.

1906    The Pekin Stock Company of Chicago formed by Robert T. Motts; Charles Gilpin in company headed by J. Edward Green; company disbanded in 1909.

1915    The Lafayette Players established by Anita Bush in Harlem; company finally disbanded in Los Angeles in 1932. Scott Joplin's opera *Treemonisha* completed but unable to secure professional production.

1917    Ridgely Torrence's *Three Plays for a Negro Theatre* reintroduces Black actors to the legitimate Broadway professional stage.

1920    Charles Gilpin stars as Brutus Jones in Eugene O'Neill's *The Emperor Jones* at Provincetown Playhouse, New York City.

1920-1950  During this period repeated attempts are made to establish a viable Black theatre company in Harlem; among the most notable efforts are the Krigwa Players (1926), Harlem Experimental Theatre (1928), Harlem Suitcase Theatre (1937), Rose McClendon Players (1938), and American Negro Theatre (1940).

1921    *Shuffle Along,* the Miller/Lyles, Sissle/Blake hit musical comedy, enjoys record run on Broadway. Howard University (Washington, D.C.) establishes a Department of Dramatic Art.

1923    Willis Richardson's one-act drama *The Chip Woman's Fortune,* first nonmusical play by a Black playwright on Broadway.

1924    Paul Robeson plays lead in Eugene O'Neill's *All God's Chillun Got Wings* produced by the Provincetown Players; interracial casting generates considerable controversy.

1926    The Krigwa Players, intended as a nationwide movement of little theatres presenting Black plays primarily for Black audiences, started by W. E. B. DuBois, editor of *The Crisis.*

Paul Green wins Pulitzer Prize for his play *In Abraham's Bosom,* with leading Black actors Rose McClendon, Abbie Mitchell, Frank Wilson, and Jules Bledsoe.

1930    The Negro Inter-Collegiate Drama Association formed by Randolph Edmonds to promote dramatic art among member colleges in the South. Marc Connelly's *The Green Pastures* opens on Broadway with an all-Black cast of some 100 actors and the Hall Johnson Choir singing Negro Spirituals; Richard B. Harrison gives towering performance as De Lawd.

1935    Langston Hughes's *Mulatto* opens on Broadway and establishes a record run for a straight play by a Black writer. The Federal Theatre Project of the Works Progress Administration, through its Negro units in several cities, provides employment for Black theatre artists and technicians during the Great Depression; the project is discontinued in 1939.

1940    The American Negro Theatre founded by Abram Hill and Fred O'Neal; greatest success (which causes its decline) is *Anna Lucasta,* produced in 1944.

1941    *Native Son* by Richard Wright (with Paul Green) produced on Broadway with Canada Lee as Bigger Thomas.

1946    Theodore Ward's *Our Lan'* opens off-Broadway at the Henry Street Playhouse and moves to the Royale Theatre for a limited run.

1953    *Take a Giant Step* by Louis Peterson enjoys critical success on Broadway.

1954    *In Splendid Error* by William Branch opens at Greenwich Mews Theatre in New York; the play contrasts the characters of Frederick Douglass and John Brown against the background of the Harper's Ferry incident.

1957    Loften Mitchell's *A Land Beyond the River* at the Greenwick Mews Theatre confronts the most pressing issue of the day: public school desegregation.

1958    Lorraine Hansberry's first play, *A Raisin in the Sun,* directed by Lloyd Richards, opens in New York to wide critical and popular acclaim; it brings Black audiences to professional Broadway theatre.

1959    *The Blacks* by Jean Genet, in a powerful production by Gene Frankel at the off-Broadway St. Mark's Playhouse, introduces the theatre of audience vilification.

1964          *Dutchman* by LeRoi Jones (Amiri Baraka) at the Cherry Lane
              Theatre off-Broadway, along with Jones's manifesto "The
              Revolutionary Theatre," heralds the Black revolutionary
              drama of the sixties.

1967-         A resurgence of Black community theatre groups around the
present       country, most notably in Boston, Buffalo, Chicago, Cleve-
              land, Detroit, Los Angeles, New Orleans, New York, Phila-
              delphia, and Washington, D.C.

1967          The Negro Ensemble Company established with Douglas
              Turner Ward as artistic director at the St. Mark's Playhouse
              in downtown New York. The New Lafayette Theatre founded
              in Harlem with Robert Macbeth as artistic director and Ed
              Bullins as playwright in residence; disbanded in 1972.

1968          The National Black Theatre formed in Harlem by Barbara
              Ann Teer; concentrates on Black communal ritual theatre as
              advocated by writers like Carlton Molette and Paul Carter
              Harrison. James Earl Jones awarded the Antoinette Perry
              Award ("Tony") for his performance as Jack Johnson in
              Howard Sackler's play *The Great White Hope.*

1970          *Ceremonies in Dark Old Men* by Lonnie Elder III just misses,
              and *No Place to Be Somebody* by Charles Gordone wins the
              Pulitzer Prize for the best American play.

1971          *El Hajj Malik* by N. R. Davidson, a play about Malcolm X,
              directed by Ernie McClintock for his Afro-American Studio
              Theatre in New York, typifies the best of the sociopolitical
              theatre presented by scores of Black theatre groups through-
              out the United States.

1970s         Lavish Black musicals once again attracting huge interracial
              audiences to Broadway; among popular attractions are
              *Purlie, Raisin, Bubbling Brown Sugar, The Wiz, Don't
              Bother Me I Can't Cope, Your Arms Too Short to Box With
              God,* and *Timbuktu!* The New York Shakespeare Public
              Theatre establishes Black and Hispanic Shakespeare
              companies.

# Notes on the Editor and Contributors

ERROL HILL is John D. Willard Professor of Drama and Oratory at Dartmouth College. A published playwright, play director, and actor, he is also the author of *The Trinidad Carnival: Mandate for a National Theatre* (1972) and editor of several collections of Caribbean plays. His articles have appeared in *Theatre Survey, Caribbean Quarterly, Cultures,* and the *Bulletin of Black Theatre* of which he was former editor for the American Theatre Association.

ERIC BENTLEY was Brander Matthews Professor of Dramatic Literature at Columbia University for sixteen years and drama critic of *The New Republic.* A recipient of the George Jean Nathan Award for drama criticism, he is author of several books on the theatre, and a playwright, editor, and adapter and translator of plays.

TOM DENT is a native of New Orleans whose journeys include *Umbra* (New York), 1962-65, the Free Southern Theater (New Orleans), 1965-70, and BLKARTSOUTH, 1969-70. He has published articles on theatre and the Black cultural movement in the South, plays, poetry, and short stories. He is coeditor of *Free Southern Theater by the Free Southern Theater* (1970) and author of *Magnolia Street* (1976).

ELLEN FOREMAN is contributing editor and theatre critic for *The Black American* newspaper in New York. Her work has appeared in *College English,* the *New York Recorder,* the *Daily Challenge, Our Town,* and the *Cleveland Press.* She teaches English at Queens College, City University of New York.

JESSICA B. HARRIS teaches at Queens College, New York, and has conducted theatre research in West Africa. She was theatre critic for the *New York Amsterdam News* and is currently a contributing editor of *Essence* magazine.

ABIODUN JEYIFOUS is a Nigerian who has taught at the City College of New York. He is currently an assistant professor of drama at the University of Ife, Ile-Ife, Nigeria. He describes himself as a socialist and pan-Africanist.

STANLEY KAUFFMANN is an author, editor, and film and theatre critic. He is a recipient of the George Jean Nathan Award for drama criticism and holds a distinguished professorship at the City University of New York.

ADAM DAVID MILLER is an instructor of English at Laney College in Oakland, California, and a teacher-consultant of the Bay Area Writing Project at the University of California, Berkeley. He is a regular contributor of articles, reviews, and verse to anthologies and periodicals.

LARRY NEAL coedited *Black Fire* (1968) with LeRoi Jones (Amiri Baraka). He was formerly arts editor of *Liberator* magazine, editor of *The Cricket,* and a contributing editor of the *Journal of Black Poetry.*

LINDSAY PATTERSON, a native of Bastrop, Louisiana, has published seven books, including *A Rock Against the Wind: Black Love Poems, Black Films and Film-makers,* and *Black Theater: A 20th Century Collection of Its Best Works.* Formerly cohost of a radio and television show in New York City, Mr. Patterson began hosting a network television series in January 1979. He is currently completing his autobiography, *Diary of an Ageing Young Writer,* and a novel.

THOMAS D. PAWLEY is dean of the College of Arts and Science and chairman of the Department of Speech and Theatre at Lincoln University, Jefferson City, Missouri. An accomplished playwright, Professor Pawley has published extensively, one of his major works being *The Black Teacher and the Dramatic Arts* (1970), which he coedited with William Reardon.

RONALD ROSS is admissions coordinator at Central City Center, Los Angeles. He formerly lectured at California State Polytechnic University, Pomona, and the University of Southern California.

SISTER M. FRANCESCA THOMPSON is the daughter of the late Edward Thompson and Evelyn Preer, members of the original Lafayette Players. Presently associate professor of theatre at Marian College in Indianapolis, she frequently lectures around the country.

ETHEL PITTS WALKER, a native of Tulsa, Oklahoma, has taught at Southern University, Baton Rouge, Louisiana, and Lincoln University, Jefferson City, Missouri, and is presently on the faculty of the University of Illinois, Urbana-Champaign.

MARGARET B. WILKERSON teaches in the Department of Afro-American Studies at the University of California, Berkeley, and is director of the Center for the Continuing Education of Women at that institution. She is active in the Northern California Black Theatre Alliance and serves as vice-chairperson of the Black Theatre Program of the American Theatre Association.

# Selected Bibliography

## I. General Works on Black Theater and Its Participants

Abramson, Doris. *Negro Playwrights in the American Theatre, 1925-1959.* New York: Columbia University Press, 1969.

American Society of African Culture. *The American Negro Writer and His Roots: Selected Papers from the First Conference of Negro Writers* (March 1959). New York, 1960.

*The American Theatre: A Sum of Its Parts.* New York: Samuel French, 1971.

Archer, Leonard C. *Black Images in American Theatre.* Nashville, Tenn.: Pageant Press, 1973.

Belcher, Fannin S., Jr. "The Place of the Negro in the Evolution of the American Theatre, 1767 to 1940." Ph.D. dissertation, Yale University, 1945

Benston, Kimberly W. *Baraka: The Renegade and the Mask.* New Haven: Yale University Press, 1976.

Bigsby, C. W. E., ed. *The Black American Writer,* Vol. II *(Poetry and Drama).* Florida: Everett/Edwards, 1969.

Bond, Frederick W. *The Negro and the Drama.* Washington, D.C.: Associated Publishers, 1940.

Brown, Sterling. *Negro Poetry and Drama.* Washington, D.C.: Associates in Negro Folk Education, 1937; reprint—New York: Atheneum, 1969.

Bullins, Ed, ed. *Black Theatre* (magazine). New York: New Lafayette Theatre, 1968-1972.

Charters, Ann. *Nobody: The Story of Bert Williams.* New York: Macmillan, 1970.

Cruse, Harold. *The Crisis of the Negro Intellectual.* New York: William Morrow, 1967.

Dent, Thomas C., Richard Schechner, and Gilbert Moses. *The Free Southern Theater by the Free Southern Theater.* Indianapolis: Bobbs-Merrill, 1969.

*The Drama Review,* Vol. 12, No. 4 (T-40, Summer 1968). The entire issue is devoted to Black theatre.

————, Vol. 16, No. 4 (T-56, December 1972). Black theatre issue.

Emery, Lynne Fauley. *Black Dance in the United States from 1619 to 1970.* Palo Alto, Calif.: National Press Books, 1972.

Farrison, William Edward. *William Wells Brown: Author and Reformer.* Chicago: University of Chicago Press, 1969.

Flannigan, Hallie. *Arena: The History of the Federal Theatre.* New York: Duell, Sloan, and Pearce, 1940.

Fletcher, Tom. *One Hundred Years of the Negro in Show Business.* New York: Burdge, 1954.

Gayle, Addison, Jr., ed. *The Black Aesthetic.* New York: Doubleday, 1971.

————, ed. *Black Expression: Essays by and about Black Americans in the Creative Arts.* New York: Weybright and Talley, 1969.

Goldstein, Rhoda L., ed. *Black Life and Culture in the United States.* New York: Thomas Y. Crowell, 1971.

Harrison, Paul Carter. *The Drama of Nommo.* New York: Grove Press, 1972.

Hatch, James V. *Black Image on the American Stage: A Bibliography of Plays and Musicals, 1770-1970.* New York: Drama Book Specialists, 1970.

————, and Omanii Abdullah. *Black Playwrights, 1823-1977: An Annotated Bibliography of Plays.* New York: R. R. Bowker, 1977.

Hill, Herbert, ed. *Anger and Beyond: The Negro Writer in the United States.* New York: Harper & Row, 1966.

Hudson, Theodore R. *From LeRoi Jones to Amiri Baraka: The Literary Works.* Durham, N.C.: Duke University Press, 1973.

Hughes, Langston, and Milton Meltzer. *Black Magic: A Pictorial History of the Negro in American Entertainment.* Englewood Cliffs, N.J.: Prentice-Hall, 1967.

Isaacs, Edith J. R. *The Negro in the American Theatre.* New York: Theatre Arts, 1947.

Jahn, Janheinz. *Muntu: An Outline of the New African Culture.* New York: Grove Press, 1961.

Johnson, James Weldon. *Black Manhattan.* New York: Alfred Knopf, 1930; reprint—New York: Atheneum, 1968.

Keil, Charles. *Urban Blues.* Chicago: University of Chicago Press, 1966.

Kimball, Robert, and William Bolcom. *Reminiscing with Sissle and Blake.* New York: Viking Press, 1973.

King, Woodie, and Earl Anthony, eds. *Black Poets and Prophets: The Theory, Practice, and Esthetics of the Pan-Africanist Revolution.* New York: New American Library, 1972.

Locke, Alain, ed. *The New Negro.* New York: Albert and Charles Boni, 1925; reprint—New York: Atheneum, 1969.

Lovell, John, Jr. *Black Song: The Forge and the Flame.* New York: Macmillan, 1972.

Marshall, Herbert, and Mildred Stock. *Ira Aldridge: The Negro Tragedian.* Carbondale: Southern Illinois University Press, 1968.

Mathews, Jane DeHart. *The Federal Theatre, 1935-1939.* Princeton, N.J.: Princeton University Press, 1967.

Meltzer, Milton. *Langston Hughes: A Biography.* New York: Thomas Y. Crowell, 1968.

Mitchell, Loften. *Black Drama: The Story of the American Negro in the Theatre.* New York: Hawthorn Books, 1967.

———. *Voices of the Black Theatre.* Clifton, N.J.: James T. White, 1975.

O'Daniel, Therman B., ed. *Langston Hughes, Black Genius: A Critical Evaluation.* New York: William Morrow, 1971.

Patterson, Lindsay. *Anthology of the American Negro in the Theatre.* New York: Publishers Company, 1967.

Robeson, Eslanda Goode. *Paul Robeson: Negro.* London: Victor Gollancz, 1930.

Sandle, Floyd L. *The Negro in the American Educational Theatre.* Ann Arbor, Mich.: Edward Brothers, 1964.

Southern, Eileen. *The Music of Black Americans: A History.* New York: W. W. Norton, 1971.

Stearns, Marshall, and Jean Stearns. *Jazz Dance: The Story of American Vernacular Dance.* New York: Macmillan, 1968.

Toll, Robert C. *Blacking Up: The Minstrel Show in Nineteenth-Century America.* New York: Oxford University Press, 1974.

Wittke, Carl. *Tambo and Bones: A History of the American Minstrel Stage.* Durham, N.C.: Duke University Press, 1930; reprint—New York: Greenwood Press, 1968.


## *II. Play Anthologies*

Baraka, Amiri (LeRoi Jones). *The Baptism and The Toilet.* New York: Grove Press, 1963, 1966.

————. *Dutchman and The Slave.* New York: William Morrow, 1964.

————. *Four Black Revolutionary Plays.* Indianapolis: Bobbs-Merrill, 1969.

————. *The Motion of History and Other Plays.* New York: William Morrow, 1978.

————, and Larry Neal, eds. *Black Fire: An Anthology of Afro-American Writing.* New York: William Morrow, 1968.

*A Black Quartet: Four New Black Plays by Ben Caldwell, Ronald Milner, Ed Bullins, and LeRoi Jones.* New York: New American Library, 1970.

Brasmer, William, and Dominick Consolo., eds. *Black Drama: An Anthology.* Columbus, Ohio: Merrill, 1970.

Brown, Sterling, Arthur Davis, and Ulysses Lee. *Negro Caravan.* New York: Dryden Press, 1941.

Bullins, Ed. *Five Plays.* Indianapolis: Bobbs-Merrill, 1969.

————. *Four Dynamite Plays.* New York: William Morrow, 1972.

————. *New Plays from the Black Theater.* New York: Bantam Books, 1969.

————. *The Theme Is Blackness.* New York: William Morrow, 1973.

————, ed. *The New Lafayette Theatre Presents: Plays with Aesthetic Comments by Six Black Playwrights.* New York: Anchor Press/Doubleday, 1974.

Childress, Alice, ed. *Black Scenes.* New York: Doubleday, 1971.

Couch, William, Jr., ed. *New Black Playwrights: An Anthology.* Baton Rouge: Louisiana State University Press, 1968.

Edmonds, Randolph. *The Land of Cotton and Other Plays.* Washington, D.C.: Associated Publishers, 1943.

―――. *Shades and Shadows*. Boston: Meador, 1930.

―――. *Six Plays for a Negro Theatre*. Boston: Walter H. Baker, 1934.

Hansberry, Lorraine. *Les Blancs: The Collected Last Plays of Lorraine Hansberry*, ed. Robert Nemiroff. New York: Random House, 1972.

―――. *A Raisin in the Sun; The Sign in Sidney Brustein's Window*. New York: New American Library, 1966.

Harrison, Paul Carter, ed. *Kuntu Drama: Plays of the African Continuum*. New York: Grove Press, 1974.

Hatch, James V., ed. *Black Theater, U.S.A.: Forty-five Plays by Black Americans, 1847-1974*. New York: Free Press, 1974.

Hughes, Langston. *Five Plays*, ed. Webster Smalley. Bloomington, Ind.: Indiana University Press, 1968.

Jones, LeRoi—*see* Baraka, Amiri.

King, Woodie, and Ron Milner, eds. *Black Drama Anthology*. New York: New American Library, 1971.

Locke, Alain, and Montgomery Gregory, eds. *Plays of Negro Life*. New York: Harper, 1927.

Oliver, Clinton, and Stephanie Sills, eds. *Contemporary Black Drama*. New York: Charles Scribner's Sons, 1971.

Patterson, Lindsay, ed. *Black Theater*. New York: Dodd, Mead, 1971.

Reardon, William, and Thomas Pawley. *The Black Teacher and the Dramatic Arts*. Westport, Conn.: Negro Universities Press, 1970.

Richardson, Willis. *The King's Dilemma and Other Plays for Children*. New York: Exposition Press, 1956.

―――, ed. *Plays and Pageants from the Life of the Negro*. Washington, D.C.: Associated Publishers, 1930.

―――, and May Miller, eds. *Negro History in Thirteen Plays*. Washington, D.C.: Associated Publishers, 1935.

Turner, Darwin T., ed. *Black Drama in America: An Anthology*. Greenwich, Conn.: Fawcett Publications, 1971.

Ward, Douglas Turner. *Two Plays: Happy Ending and Day of Absence*. New York: Third Press, 1966.

White, Edgar. *Underground: Four Plays*. New York: William Morrow, 1970.